CYPRUS TRAVEL GUIDE 2023

Uncover the beauty of Cyprus: Island of Love

SOLOMON LEWIS

Copyrights

All rights reserved. No part may be reproduced, distributed or transmitted in any form or by any means, including photocopying, recording, or other electronic or mechanical methods without the prior written permission of the publisher, except in the case of brief quotation embodied in critical reviews and certain other non-commercial uses permitted by copyright law

Copyright © SOLOMON LEWIS, 2023

Table of Contents

Introduction
- Welcome to Cyprus
- About this Guide
- Is Cyprus Safe

Chapter 1: Things to Know Before Coming
- Culture and Etiquette in Cyprus
  - Dating Culture in Cyprus
- How to dress in Cyprus
- Driving in Cyprus

Chapter 2: General Information
- Geography and Climate
- History and Culture
- Language and Currency
- Getting Around in Cyprus
- Accommodation Options

Chapter 3: Top Destinations in Cyprus

Nicosia
- Top Attractions
- Where to Eat
- Nightlife
- Day Trip from Nicosia
- Where to Relax and Enjoy

Limassol
- Top attractions
- Where to Eat
- Nightlife
- Day trip from Limassol
- Where Relax and Enjoy

Paphos
- Top attractions
- Where to Eat
- Paphos Nightlife
- Day trip from Paphos
- Where to Relax and Enjoy

Larnaca
- Top Attractions
- Where to Eat
- Larnaca Nightlife
- Day trip from Larnaca
- Where Relax and Enjoy

Ayia Napa
- Top Attractions
- Where to Eat
- Ayia Napa Nightlife
- Day trip from Ayia Napa
- Where Relax and Enjoy

Chapter 4: Shopping
- Souvenirs and Local Products
- Markets and Shopping Centers

Chapter 5: Best Activities
- Beaches and What they Offer
- Historic Sites
- Museums and Galleries

Outdoor Activities

Chapter 6: Food and Drink

   Cypriot Cuisine

   Popular Dishes and Drinks

   Restaurants and Cafes

Chapter 7: Practical Information

   Health and Safety

   Communication and Internet

Conclusion

   Final Thoughts

   Useful Resources to plan your trip to Cyprus

Introduction

Welcome to Cyprus

Welcome to Cyprus, the jewel of the Mediterranean! With its crystal-clear waters, golden beaches, and stunning landscapes, Cyprus is the perfect destination for those seeking a mix of relaxation and adventure.

As you step foot on this beautiful island, you will be greeted with warm hospitality and a rich cultural heritage that dates back thousands of years.

From ancient ruins to modern-day wonders, Cyprus has it all.

Take a stroll through charming villages and discover traditional Cypriot architecture and crafts. Or, explore the island's history and mythology by visiting archaeological sites such as the ancient city of Kourion and the Tombs of the Kings.

Indulge in the delicious local cuisine, which draws on Greek, Turkish, and Middle Eastern influences. Savor fresh seafood, succulent meats, and a range of meze dishes that showcase the island's diverse flavors.

For the adventure seekers, Cyprus offers a plethora of activities, from water sports and hiking to mountain biking and rock climbing. With its mild climate year-round, there's never a bad time to explore the great outdoors.

As the sun sets over the Mediterranean, unwind with a refreshing drink and take in the stunning views. Whether you're looking for a romantic getaway, a family vacation, or a solo adventure, Cyprus is sure to captivate you with its beauty and charm.

As you settle into the pace of life in Cyprus, you'll discover that the island has a unique way of blending traditional culture with modern amenities. You can find everything from luxury resorts to quaint guesthouses, and bustling cities to quiet villages, all with their own distinct personalities.

One of the best ways to experience the island's beauty is to take a scenic drive along the winding coastal roads. Stop at hidden beaches and seaside tavernas along the way, and enjoy the stunning views of the Mediterranean sea.

If you're a nature lover, you'll be in paradise on this island. From the stunning Akamas Peninsula to the Troodos mountains, Cyprus boasts a diverse landscape with plenty of opportunities for hiking and exploring. You can even go on a wildflower tour and discover the island's vibrant flora and fauna.

For those looking for a more urban experience, the cities of Nicosia, Limassol, and Larnaca offer a vibrant mix of history, culture, and entertainment. Explore the medieval streets of Nicosia's old town, shop for souvenirs in Limassol's modern malls, or hit the clubs in Larnaca's buzzing nightlife scene.

Welcome to Cyprus, where the past meets the present, and every moment is a treasure to be cherished

About this Guide

The Cyprus Travel Guide is an extensive guidebook that offers a comprehensive overview of one of the most popular tourist destinations in the Mediterranean.

The guide provides visitors with detailed information about the island nation of Cyprus, including its history, culture, cuisine, and top attractions. Whether you're planning a romantic getaway, a family vacation, or an adventure-filled trip, the Cyprus Travel Guide is an indispensable resource that will help you make the most of your time on the island.

The guide is divided into several sections that cover everything from the basics of getting to Cyprus to the finer details of local customs and etiquette. The first section provides an overview of the island's geography, climate, and history. It also offers practical advice on how to plan your trip, including when to visit, how to get around, and where to stay.

The second section of the guide is dedicated to the island's top attractions. From ancient ruins and museums to beautiful beaches and natural parks, Cyprus offers a wealth of sights and experiences for visitors to enjoy. The guide provides detailed descriptions of each attraction, along with tips on how to get the most out of your visit.

The third section of the guide focuses on the island's cuisine and local specialties. Cyprus has a rich culinary tradition, with a variety of dishes that reflect its history and cultural influences. The guide provides an overview of the island's cuisine, as well as recommendations on where to sample the best food and drink.

In addition to the sections mentioned above, the Cyprus Travel Guide also provides useful information on outdoor activities, such as hiking, cycling, and watersports. Cyprus boasts a stunning natural landscape, with picturesque villages, rugged mountains, and crystal-clear waters. The guide offers detailed information on the best places to explore, as well as tips on equipment rental, safety, and environmental considerations.

For those interested in the island's cultural heritage, the guide includes a section on traditional arts and crafts. Cyprus has a long and rich tradition of handicrafts, such as pottery, weaving, and embroidery. Visitors can learn more about these crafts by visiting local workshops and museums, and the guide provides helpful tips on where to find them.

Another important feature of the Cyprus Travel Guide is its accommodation section. Cyprus has a wide range of accommodation options, from luxury resorts and boutique hotels to budget-friendly hostels and apartments. The guide provides detailed descriptions of each type of accommodation, as well as tips on how to find the best deals and make reservations.

Overall, the Cyprus Travel Guide is a comprehensive and well-researched resource that will help visitors get the most out of their trip to this beautiful island nation. Whether you're interested in history, culture, cuisine, or outdoor activities, the guide has something to offer everyone. With its practical advice, insider tips, and detailed information, the Cyprus Travel Guide is a must-have for any traveler planning a visit to this fascinating destination.

Is Cyprus Safe

Cyprus is generally considered to be a safe country for tourists and locals alike. The country has a low crime rate and a stable political environment, making it a popular destination for visitors from around the world.

Safety in Cyprus is a top priority for the government, and the country has implemented several measures to ensure the safety and security of its residents and visitors. There is a strong police presence throughout the country, and the police force is generally well-equipped and professional.

In terms of crime, Cyprus has a relatively low crime rate compared to other European countries. Petty crime such as pickpocketing and theft can occur in tourist areas, but these incidents are rare and can be avoided by taking basic precautions such as keeping valuables out of sight and securing your belongings.

Cyprus is also a popular destination for families, and there are many family-friendly activities and attractions throughout the country. The beaches in Cyprus are generally safe for swimming, and the country has a high standard of healthcare facilities.

While Cyprus is generally considered to be a safe country, there are some areas where caution should be taken. The northern part of the island is currently occupied by Turkish forces, and visitors are advised to avoid this area due to the potential for conflict. In addition, visitors should exercise caution when traveling to border areas, as there have been incidents of violence in the past.

Cyprus is also located in a seismically active region, and earthquakes can occur. The government has implemented measures to ensure that buildings and infrastructure are built to withstand earthquakes, but visitors should be aware of this potential risk.

In terms of terrorism, Cyprus has a low risk of terrorist activity, but visitors should remain vigilant and report any suspicious activity to the authorities.

Cyprus also has a well-developed transport system, including buses, taxis, and rental cars. However, visitors should be aware that driving in Cyprus can be challenging due to the country's narrow and winding roads, as well as the need to drive on the left side of the road. Visitors should also be aware of the risk of drunk driving, which is a significant problem in Cyprus.

While Cyprus is generally safe, visitors should also be aware of the potential for natural disasters, such as forest fires and flash floods. Visitors should monitor local weather conditions and heed any warnings issued by the authorities.

In terms of health, Cyprus has a high standard of healthcare facilities and medical care is generally readily available. Visitors should ensure that they have adequate health insurance to cover any medical expenses during their stay.

Cyprus is generally considered to be a safe country with a low crime rate and stable political environment. Visitors should exercise common sense and take basic precautions to ensure their safety, but can generally expect a safe and enjoyable experience in Cyprus.

Chapter 1: Things to Know Before Coming

Culture and Etiquette in Cyprus

It's good to know you are not violating any laws or disrespecting inhabitants while going to a new nation. The people of Cyprus want to respect tradition, and they are courteous when it comes to what is proper in social circumstances. When compared to other areas in Europe, it is significantly different. Below is the list of the Cyprus Culture, Traditions, and Etiquette.

Religion in Cyprus

The Cyprus constitution protects freedom of religion, despite the country being primarily Christian and Muslim. The Greek Orthodox Church is attended by the majority of Greek Cypriots. One of the first autocephalous churches, the Church of Cyprus recognizes the ecumenical patriarch in Constantinople and retains administrative independence under the leadership of its archbishop.

Women attend church services more consistently than males do in small towns, and senior family members generally fulfill family-wide religious commitments. In cities and among Cypriots with higher education, church attendance is less prevalent. Most people's religious traditions focus on family rituals, idol worship, and observance of some Orthodox feast days. Muslims make up the majority of Turkish Cypriots.

Muslims are supposed to do five daily prayers at dawn, noon, afternoon, sunset, and nighttime. All Muslims are obligated to fast from dawn until dark and are only permitted to work six hours a day during the holy month of Ramadan. A person who is fasting refrains from eating, drinking, smoking, and chewing gum. Outsiders are not obliged to fast, but they are barred from eating, drinking, smoking, or chewing gum in public.

Family Values and Society

The social system is oriented toward the family. The family is made up of both immediate and extended relatives. It is anticipated that the extended family would aid the relatives. Grandfathers, both paternal and maternal, appreciate tight ties with their grandchildren.

Children are expected to care for their parents when they age or grow sick, and seniors are valued. Due to their two principal religions, Greek Orthodox in Greek Cyprus and Islam in Turkish Cyprus, Cypriots have a profound respect for authority. Individuals are cherished regardless of their position and age. Elderly persons are revered and considered wise. In a group, the senior member is revered and recognized. They are served and introduced initially in a social situation.

Families typically dine together at restaurants or at home in Cyprus, where the focus is still very much on the family. This is particularly true on Sundays. It is fairly typical to see multiple automobiles unload large families, including the elderly, teenagers, and children, onto the beach or at picnic spots. The families then go on to set up barbecues, play music on portable sound systems, and settle in for the day.

Respect for the elderly, compassion for expecting moms, and indulgence for kids are all regularly practiced. Owing in part to an ancient wives' tradition that suggests that if pregnant ladies don't obtain what they want to eat, their unborn child would be birth-marked appropriately, pregnant women are given extra attention.

Cypriots who enquire about your kids or grandkids aren't merely being polite; they want to know. So answer them and enquire back.

Manners

While offering a welcome, shake hands, smile, and establish direct eye contact. During the welcome, a lot of Turkish Cypriots avert their gaze out of respect. Muslims who practice extreme piety avoid shaking hands with women. Before addressing someone by their first name, wait to be invited. Your hosts will introduce you to the other guests at special social events. While departing, say goodbye to each individual separately.

This is one of the top things to know about Cyprus Culture, Traditions, and Etiquette. Presenting presents is not a complex task. If you are welcomed to a Cypriot's house, bring a culinary present, like pastries. White lilies are not suited as funeral flowers. When received, presents are not always opened. While visiting a Cypriot's house after being invited, shake hands with everyone upon arriving and departing. Dress elegantly yet casually. Offer to help the hostess with the meal's preparation or cleaning afterward.

Dining Etiquette

While visiting a Cypriot's home after being invited, shake hands with everyone upon arriving and departing. They dress nicely yet casually. Offer to help the hostess with the meal's preparation or cleaning afterward.
Continental table manners dictate that the knife should be held in the right hand while eating and the fork in the left. Unless you are instructed to sit down and maintain standing. Normally,

the oldest person and guest of honor have first dibs.

You should wait until the hostess begins to eat before commencing. Use just your right hand to pass dishes. Anticipate getting extra portions, maybe even a third. Eating everything on your plate is considered respectful. Cross your knife and fork on your plate, the fork passing over the knife, if you haven't done eating. Placing your knife and fork parallel over the right side of your dish implies that you are done eating.

Tipping Etiquette

Tipping Etiquette is one of the top things to know about Cyprus's Culture, Traditions, and Etiquette Tipping is quite common in Cyprus because it is a major tourist destination. It's not necessary, so there won't be an issue if you opt not to tip due to bad service. If there is a service fee on your account, you shouldn't give a tip. 3-4 Euros should be adequate as a tip on invoices without a service fee.

While most service providers do not expect gratuities, it is always appreciated if you do. Round up your taxi bill or add a few euros for the porters or housekeepers, and then do the same for your driver. You should be aware that it's exceedingly unusual for any tips you leave on your card to reach the server. Be sure to take cash and tip the server personally.

Dating Culture in Cyprus

Dating culture in Cyprus is an interesting mix of traditional and modern practices. In this article, we will discuss the various aspects of dating culture in Cyprus.

Traditional Dating Culture

In Cyprus, traditional dating culture is still prevalent in some parts of the country. The traditional way of dating involves meeting through family, friends, or in social gatherings. Cypriot families are typically close-knit, and it is common for parents to introduce their children to potential partners.

In traditional dating, the man is expected to take the lead and ask the woman out. The first date is usually a casual meeting where the couple gets to know each other. In traditional dating culture, the woman is expected to be modest and conservative. It is also common for the man to pay for the date.

Modern Dating Culture

The dating culture in Cyprus has evolved over the years, and modern dating practices are becoming more common. Online dating has become a popular way to meet new people in Cyprus. Dating apps such as Tinder, Badoo, and OkCupid are widely used in the country.

Modern dating culture in Cyprus is more relaxed than traditional dating. Men and women have equal opportunities to initiate a conversation and ask each other out. In modern dating, the first date is often a casual meeting in a coffee shop or a bar. Splitting the bill is becoming more common, especially among younger generations.

Dating Etiquette

Regardless of whether you are dating in a traditional or modern way, there are some dating etiquette rules to follow in Cyprus. Cypriot culture values respect and politeness, and these values are reflected in dating etiquette.

One of the most important rules of dating etiquette in Cyprus is to be punctual. Cypriots value timekeeping and being late for a date is considered disrespectful. Dressing appropriately for the occasion is also important. Cypriots take pride in their appearance, and dressing well for a date is a sign of respect.

Another important dating etiquette rule is to avoid discussing politics or religion on a first date. These topics can be sensitive and may cause disagreements. It is better to focus on getting to know each other and finding common ground.

Dating in Cyprus is also influenced by the country's conservative values and strong family ties. It is common for families to be involved in the dating process, and it is important to respect the opinions and wishes of your partner's family.

One interesting aspect of dating culture in Cyprus is the concept of "filotimo," which roughly translates to "love of honor." This concept is deeply ingrained in Cypriot culture and refers to the idea of doing what is right and honorable. It is important to show respect, honesty, and kindness in relationships, and to behave in a way that reflects well on yourself and your family.

Another aspect of dating culture in Cyprus is the role of gender. While gender roles are becoming more flexible in modern society, there are still some traditional expectations when it comes to dating. Men are typically expected to take the lead and be chivalrous, while women are expected to be modest and feminine. However, these expectations are changing, and many Cypriot women are becoming more assertive in their dating lives.

In recent years, there has been a growing trend of intercultural dating in Cyprus. As the country becomes more diverse, it is becoming increasingly common for people of different cultures and backgrounds to date and form relationships. While this is generally accepted in modern society, there may still be some cultural barriers and challenges to overcome.

Overall, dating culture in Cyprus is a fascinating blend of traditional values and modern practices. Whether you prefer traditional dating or modern online dating, it is important to respect the cultural norms and values of your partner and their family. By doing so, you can build strong and meaningful relationships in this beautiful island country.

How to dress in Cyprus

When it comes to dressing in Cyprus, there are a few things to keep in mind to ensure you are comfortable and respectful of the local customs. In this article, we'll explore some tips on how to dress in Cyprus and highlight some things visitors should know about the island's dressing culture.

Firstly, it's important to note that Cyprus is a conservative country, especially when it comes to clothing. While you don't need to cover up completely, it's best to avoid revealing too much skin, especially when visiting places of worship or local villages. This means that shorts, skirts, and dresses should be knee-length or longer, and tops should cover the shoulders and chest. Swimwear is acceptable on the beach or at a resort, but it's best to cover up when leaving these areas.

Another important thing to keep in mind is the weather. Cyprus enjoys a hot and dry Mediterranean climate, with temperatures often reaching 30 degrees Celsius (86 degrees Fahrenheit) or higher during the summer months. Lightweight, breathable fabrics like cotton, linen, and rayon are ideal for staying cool and comfortable. Avoid heavy materials like denim or wool, which can be uncomfortable in the heat.

When it comes to footwear, sandals or comfortable walking shoes are a must for exploring the island's cities and beaches. High heels may be suitable for a night out, but they can be difficult to walk in on the cobblestone streets found in many Cypriot villages.

Additionally, it's a good idea to bring a hat and sunglasses to protect yourself from the strong sun.

Cyprus has a rich history and culture, and traditional clothing can still be seen in some areas. In particular, you may come across men wearing the "vraka," a baggy pair of trousers made from a lightweight fabric like cotton or linen. Women may wear colorful dresses, often with intricate embroidery and lace. While it's not necessary to wear traditional clothing, it can be a fun way to immerse yourself in Cypriot culture and make some local friends.

Another thing to consider when dressing in Cyprus is the time of day. While the island has a relaxed atmosphere, it's best to dress appropriately for the time of day and occasion. During the day, casual wear like shorts, t-shirts, and sundresses are suitable, while in the evening, you may want to dress up a little more for dinner or drinks.

When visiting religious sites, it's important to dress modestly out of respect for the culture and beliefs of the locals. This means covering your shoulders and knees, and avoiding wearing revealing clothing.

Additionally, it's worth noting that some religious sites may require visitors to remove their shoes before entering, so make sure to wear socks or bring a pair of easy-to-slip-on shoes.

If you're planning to hike or explore the countryside, it's important to wear appropriate clothing and footwear. Cyprus has some beautiful nature trails and hiking routes, but they can be rocky and uneven, so sturdy footwear like hiking boots is recommended. Additionally, it's a good idea to wear long pants and bring a lightweight jacket, as temperatures can drop in the mountains.

When it comes to shopping, Cyprus has a variety of markets and boutiques selling everything from souvenirs to designer clothing. However, it's important to be aware of the quality of the items you're buying, especially if you're purchasing luxury goods like handbags or watches. Make sure to check for authenticity and avoid buying from street vendors, as they may sell counterfeit items.

In terms of colors, Cyprus has a vibrant and colorful culture, and this is reflected in the clothing worn by locals. Bright colors and bold patterns are popular, especially during festivals and celebrations. If you're feeling adventurous, don't be afraid to experiment with color and pattern in your own wardrobe.

In conclusion, dressing in Cyprus is all about finding a balance between comfort and respect for local customs. By keeping in mind the climate, cultural expectations, and activities you have planned, you can ensure that you're dressed appropriately for any occasion. Remember to be respectful, stay cool in the heat, and enjoy everything that this beautiful island has to offer.

Driving in Cyprus

One of the best ways to explore Cyprus is by driving, as it allows you to see all the sights at your own pace and in your own time. In this article, we will discuss everything you need to know about driving in Cyprus, including the rules of the road, driving conditions, and some tips to help you stay safe on the road.

Driving Rules and Regulations in Cyprus:

To drive legally in Cyprus, you must have a valid driving license from your home country, which you will need to carry with you at all times. Cyprus has a system of left-hand driving, which can be confusing for those used to right-hand driving. You should always drive on the left side of the road and overtake on the right.

Speed limits in Cyprus are in kilometers per hour, and they are as follows:

50 km/h in urban areas

80 km/h on rural roads

100 km/h on highways

Seatbelts are mandatory for both drivers and passengers, and children under 5 years old must be in a child seat. The use of mobile phones while driving is prohibited, and you will be fined if you are caught.

Drunk driving is strictly prohibited in Cyprus, and the legal blood alcohol limit is 0.05%. If you are caught driving under the influence of alcohol, you will face a hefty fine, and your driving license may be suspended or even revoked.

Driving Conditions in Cyprus:

Cyprus has a relatively good road network, with most roads being well-maintained and signposted. However, there are some rural roads that can be narrow and winding, so you should take extra care when driving on them.

During the summer months, temperatures in Cyprus can soar, and this can lead to some challenging driving conditions. You should ensure that your car is properly equipped with air conditioning, and you should always carry plenty of water with you.

The roads in Cyprus can also be quite busy, especially during peak tourist season. You should be prepared for heavy traffic and allow plenty of time for your journeys.

Tips for Safe Driving in Cyprus:

- Familiarize yourself with the rules of the road in Cyprus before you start driving.
- Always wear your seatbelt and ensure that children are properly secured in car seats.
- Never use your mobile phone while driving.

- Be aware of the heat, and ensure that your car is properly equipped with air conditioning and that you carry plenty of water with you.
- Take extra care when driving on rural roads, which can be narrow and winding.
- Be prepared for heavy traffic, especially during peak tourist season.
- Always drive defensively and be aware of other drivers on the road.

Know the road signs and signals

Road signs in Cyprus are mostly in Greek and English. Familiarize yourself with the common road signs and signals, especially if you're not familiar with the Greek language. Also, be aware that the speed limit signs are in kilometers per hour, not miles per hour.

Be cautious of other drivers

Cyprus has a high rate of road accidents, and many of these accidents are caused by reckless drivers. Be cautious of other drivers on the road, especially motorcyclists and young drivers. Avoid tailgating, use your indicators properly, and be patient with other drivers.

Be prepared for roundabouts

Roundabouts are common in Cyprus, and they can be confusing if you're not used to them. Remember to give way to traffic already on the roundabout and always indicate when you're exiting.

Be cautious of pedestrians

Pedestrians in Cyprus have the right of way, and they often cross the road without looking both ways. Be cautious when driving in built-up areas, especially around schools and pedestrian crossings.

Be aware of parking restrictions

Parking can be challenging in Cyprus, especially in busy tourist areas. Be aware of parking restrictions, as parking illegally can result in a fine or your car being towed away.

Carry the necessary documents

When driving in Cyprus, always carry your driving license, car registration documents, and insurance documents. Police may conduct random checks, and you may face a fine if you can't produce these documents.

Plan your route

Before setting off on a journey, plan your route and check for any road closures or traffic disruptions. Cyprus has an excellent road network, but some roads may be closed due to roadworks or other events.

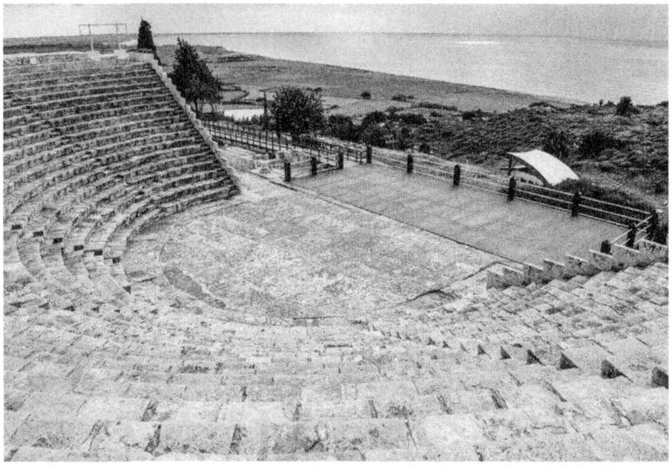

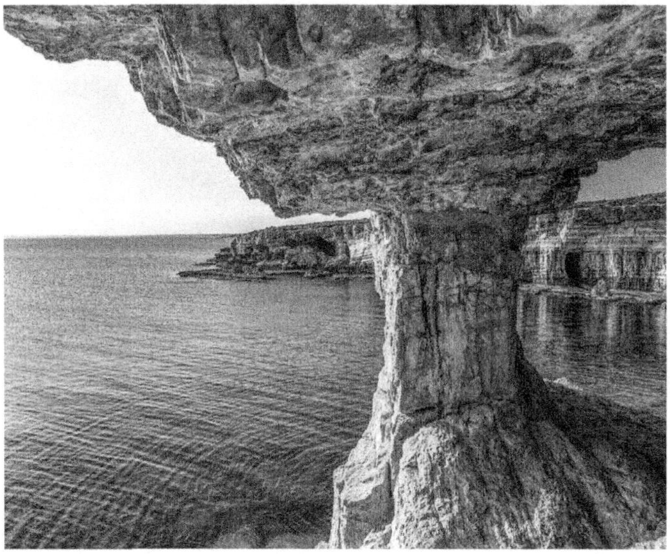

Chapter 2: General Information

Geography and Climate

Geography:

Cyprus is a mountainous island, with the Troodos Mountains occupying most of its central and western areas. The highest peak is Mount Olympus, which stands at 1,951 meters. The central plain, known as the Mesaoria, lies between the Troodos Mountains and the Kyrenia Range in the north. The Kyrenia Range is a narrow strip of mountains that runs along the northern coast of Cyprus. The island is divided into two parts, the Republic of Cyprus in the south and the Turkish Republic of Northern Cyprus in the north. The capital of the Republic of Cyprus is Nicosia, and the largest city is Limassol.

Cyprus has a complex geology, with different rock types that have been formed over millions of years. The Troodos Mountains are primarily made up of igneous rocks, such as basalt and andesite, which were formed from volcanic activity. The Kyrenia Range is composed of limestone, which was formed from the remains of ancient sea creatures. The Mesaoria plain is mainly made up of alluvial deposits, which were deposited by rivers over time.

Climate:

Cyprus has a subtropical climate, with hot and dry summers and mild winters. The island enjoys about 320 days of sunshine per year, making it an ideal destination for tourists. The hottest months are July and August, with average temperatures of around 32°C (90°F) in the coastal areas. The winter months, from December to February, are cooler, with temperatures ranging from 16°C to 18°C (61°F to 64°F) in the coastal areas.

Cyprus experiences two main seasons - the dry season from May to October, and the wet season from November to April. The island receives an average annual rainfall of around 450 millimeters, with most of the rainfall occurring during the winter months. The Troodos Mountains receive the highest amount of rainfall, with some areas receiving up to 1,000 millimeters per year. Snowfall is also common in the mountains during the winter months, and the Troodos ski resort is a popular destination for winter sports enthusiasts.

The unique geography of Cyprus also makes it an important location for agriculture. Despite the arid climate, the island has a long tradition of agriculture, with crops such as grapes, citrus, olives, and vegetables grown throughout the island. The Mesaoria plain, with its fertile alluvial soil, is the primary agricultural region, while the Troodos Mountains provide ideal conditions for vineyards and fruit trees.

In recent years, Cyprus has also become a leader in renewable energy, particularly in the development of solar power. The island's abundance of sunshine makes it an ideal location for solar energy projects, and the government has set a target of generating 13% of the country's electricity from renewable sources by 2020. The island is also exploring the potential for offshore wind power, with plans to build a wind farm off the coast of Limassol.

However, Cyprus is also facing challenges related to its geography and climate. The island is prone to droughts, and water scarcity is a significant issue, particularly during the summer months. The government has implemented various measures to address this issue, such as desalination plants and water recycling projects.

Another challenge is the threat of wildfires, particularly in the summer months when the weather is hot and dry. The government has established a dedicated firefighting force and implemented measures to prevent and respond to wildfires.

The geography and climate of Cyprus have played a significant role in shaping the island's history, culture, and economy. The island's diverse landscape, subtropical climate, and abundant sunshine make it an ideal destination for tourists and a vital location for agriculture and renewable energy. However, Cyprus also faces challenges related to water scarcity and wildfires, which require ongoing efforts to address. Despite these challenges, Cyprus remains a beautiful and unique location with much to offer visitors and residents alike.

History and Culture

History of Cyprus:

The earliest inhabitants of Cyprus were likely the Mycenaean Greeks, who arrived on the island in the 2nd millennium BC. They were followed by the Phoenicians, who established a trading post on the island in the 9th century BC. The island was subsequently conquered by the Assyrians, Egyptians, Persians, and Alexander the Great.

In the 4th century BC, Cyprus became part of the Hellenistic world, and Greek culture and language became dominant on the island. During this period, the island prospered and became a center of trade and commerce. The island was subsequently ruled by the Romans, Byzantines, and Ottomans before becoming a British colony in 1878.

During World War II, Cyprus was a strategic base for the British, and the island became a center of resistance against the Axis powers. After the war, Cyprus became a British Crown colony, and in 1960, the island gained its independence.

However, the island's history has been marked by conflict, particularly between the Greek Cypriot and Turkish Cypriot communities. In 1974, Turkey invaded the island and occupied the northern part of the island, leading to the division of the island into the internationally recognized Republic of Cyprus in the south and the unrecognized Turkish Republic of Northern Cyprus in the north.

Culture of Cyprus:

The culture of Cyprus is a blend of Greek, Turkish, and Middle Eastern influences, reflecting the island's position at the crossroads of Europe, Asia, and Africa. The island's cuisine is particularly noteworthy, featuring dishes such as kleftiko (slow-cooked lamb), stuffed grape leaves, and loukoumades (honey-soaked donut holes).

Music and dance are also important parts of Cypriot culture. The island has a rich tradition of folk music, which is characterized by the use of instruments such as the lute, violin, and accordion. The island's traditional dances include the sousta, which is performed at weddings and other celebrations.

Art and architecture are also important parts of Cypriot culture. The Byzantine Empire had a profound impact on Cypriot art and architecture, particularly in the fields of mosaics and frescoes. Many of the island's churches and monasteries date back to this period and feature intricate designs and religious themes.

Cypriot pottery is also highly regarded, with a tradition of pottery-making dating back thousands of years. The island's potters are known for their use of intricate designs and bold colors, and many of their pieces are highly prized by collectors

The Greek Orthodox Church has played a major role in the history and culture of Cyprus, with Christianity being the dominant religion on the island since the 4th century AD. Many of the island's most important religious sites, including the Monastery of Kykkos and the Church of Saint Lazarus, are associated with the Orthodox Church.

The culture of Cyprus is a blend of Greek, Turkish, and Middle Eastern influences, reflecting the island's position at the crossroads of Europe, Asia, and Africa. The island's cuisine is particularly noteworthy, featuring dishes such as souvlaki (grilled meat skewers), moussaka (a baked dish of eggplant, meat, and tomato sauce), and halloumi cheese.

Here are five historical facts about Cyprus' culture:

The island has a long tradition of wine-making, dating back over 4,000 years. Cypriot wines were highly prized in the ancient world and were even mentioned by Homer in the Iliad.

The Byzantine Empire had a profound impact on Cypriot culture, particularly in the fields of art and architecture. Many of the island's churches and monasteries date back to this period and feature intricate mosaics and frescoes.

Cyprus has a rich tradition of folk music, which is characterized by the use of instruments such as the lute, violin, and accordion. The island's traditional dances include the sousta, which is performed at weddings and other celebrations.

The island is famous for its pottery, which has been produced on the island for thousands of years. Cypriot potters are known for their use of intricate designs and bold colors.

The Greek Orthodox Church has played a major role in the history and culture of Cyprus, with Christianity being the dominant religion on the island since the 4th century AD. Many of the island's most important religious sites, including the Monastery of Kykkos and the Church of Saint Lazarus, are associated with the Orthodox Church.

Language and Currency

The official languages of Cyprus are Greek and Turkish, but English is widely spoken and understood, especially in the tourism industry. In addition, many people in Cyprus also speak other languages, such as Russian, German, and French.

Greek is the most widely spoken language in Cyprus, and it is the official language of the Greek Cypriot community. The Cypriot Greek dialect has some unique features, including a few words borrowed from Turkish and English. If you're planning to visit Cyprus, it's a good idea to learn some basic Greek phrases to help you communicate with locals.

Some common Greek phrases that may be useful for travelers in Cyprus include:

Γεια σας (Yia sas) - Hello (formal)
Γεια σου (Yia sou) - Hello (informal)
Ευχαριστώ (Efharisto) - Thank you
Παρακαλώ (Parakalo) - Please
Ναι (Nai) - Yes
Όχι (Ohi) - No
Συγγνώμη (Syngnomi) - Sorry
Τι κάνεις; (Ti kanis?) - How are you? (informal)
Τι κάνετε; (Ti kanete?) - How are you? (formal)

Μιλάτε αγγλικά; (Milate anglika?) - Do you speak English?

If you're traveling to the northern part of Cyprus, which is under Turkish control, you may find it helpful to learn some basic Turkish phrases as well. Some common Turkish phrases that may be useful for travelers in Cyprus include:

Merhaba - Hello
Teşekkür ederim - Thank you
Lütfen - Please
Evet - Yes
Hayır - No

Özür dilerim – Sorry

Nasılsın? – How are you? (informal)

Nasılsınız? – How are you? (formal)

İngilizce konuşabilir misiniz? – Do you speak English?

In addition to these basic phrases, it's also helpful to know some common words and expressions that may come up during your travels in Cyprus. Here are a few examples:

Καλημέρα (Kalimera) – Good morning

Καλησπέρα (Kalispera) – Good evening

Καληνύχτα (Kalinichta) – Good night

Πόσο κοστίζει αυτό; (Poso kostizi afto?) - How much does this cost?

Πού είναι η τουαλέτα; (Pou einai i tualeta?) - Where is the bathroom?

Μπορείτε να μου δείξετε τον δρόμο; (Boreite na mou deixete ton dromo?) - Can you show me the way?

Το μενού, παρακαλώ (To menu, parakalo) - The menu, please

Θέλω έναν καφέ (Thelo enan kafe) - I want a coffee

Πώς φτάνω στο ξενοδοχείο; (Pos ftano sto xenodocheio?) - How do I get to the hotel?

Πείνασα/ Διψάω (Peinasa/ Dipsao) - I'm hungry/ I'm thirsty

It's worth noting that in Cyprus, there are some differences in vocabulary and pronunciation between the Greek Cypriot dialect and the standard Greek language spoken in Greece. For example, the letter "γ" is pronounced like "y" in Cyprus, while in Greece it's pronounced like "g". Additionally, some words may have different meanings or connotations depending on the dialect, so it's important to be aware of these differences when communicating with locals.

Currency

Cyprus has been using the euro as its official currency since January 1, 2008. Prior to this, the official currency of Cyprus was the Cypriot pound (CYP). However, with the country's accession to the European Union in 2004, the decision was made to switch to the euro.

The euro is a common currency used by most of the countries in the European Union, and it is used by more than 340 million people as their primary currency. It is also the second most traded currency in the world, after the US dollar.

The Central Bank of Cyprus is responsible for the implementation of monetary policy in the country, and it is part of the European Central Bank (ECB) system. This means that the monetary policy decisions made by the ECB also affect Cyprus.

The exchange rate between the euro and other currencies, including the US dollar, fluctuates regularly based on various economic factors, such as inflation, interest rates, and political events. As a result, the value of the euro can rise or fall relative to other currencies, which can have an impact on international trade and investment.

Getting Around in Cyprus

Getting around Cyprus can be an exciting experience, as there are plenty of options available to explore the island's beauty. Here are some ways to get around Cyprus:

Rent a Car: Renting a car is a popular way to get around Cyprus. The roads are well-maintained, and there are plenty of car rental companies to choose from.

The major cities in Cyprus, such as Nicosia, Limassol, and Larnaca, have multiple car rental agencies that offer competitive prices. It is recommended to book in advance, especially during peak tourist season, to ensure availability. Drivers in Cyprus drive on the left-hand side of the road, and speed limits are in kilometers per hour.

Public Transportation: Public transportation in Cyprus is affordable and efficient, with a network of buses, taxis, and trains connecting major cities and towns. The main bus company in Cyprus is called "OSEL," which operates a vast network of buses that connect all major cities and towns on the island. The buses are modern, air-conditioned, and equipped with Wi-Fi. Taxis are also widely available and relatively inexpensive compared to other European countries.

Cycling: Cycling is an excellent way to explore Cyprus, especially in the coastal areas, where there are dedicated bike lanes. There are many cycling rental shops in Cyprus, particularly in the tourist areas. The island has several cycling routes, including the Cyprus Cycling Route, which is a 400 km-long path that takes you through the heart of the island.

Walking: Walking is an excellent way to explore the traditional villages and scenic countryside of Cyprus. There are several walking trails in Cyprus that range from easy to challenging. The most popular walking trails in Cyprus are the Akamas Peninsula National Park, Troodos Mountains, and the Aphrodite Trail.

Ferries: Ferries are a popular mode of transportation in Cyprus, especially for island-hopping. There are several ferry companies that operate services between Cyprus and neighboring countries, including Greece, Turkey, and Israel. The ferry journey from

Cyprus to Greece takes around 24 hours, while the journey to Turkey takes around 4-5 hours.

Cyprus has a well-developed transportation system that includes road, air, and sea transport. The transportation infrastructure is modern and well-maintained, and there are several options available for getting around the island.

Road Transport: The road transport network in Cyprus is well-developed, with a network of highways, primary and secondary roads that connect major cities and towns. The roads are well-maintained, and there are plenty of signs to help visitors navigate their way around the island. The main highways on the island are the A1, which connects Nicosia and Limassol, and the A6, which connects Limassol and Paphos. Cyprus also has a network of local buses that connect towns and cities, with the main bus company being OSEL.

Air Transport: Cyprus has two main airports, Larnaca International Airport and Paphos International Airport. Both airports offer regular flights to and from major cities in Europe and the Middle East. The airports are modern and well-equipped, with facilities such as duty-free shops, restaurants, and car rental agencies. Cyprus Airways is the national carrier and offers both domestic and international flights.

Sea Transport: Cyprus has several ports, the most significant being the Port of Limassol, which is the largest port on the island. The port serves as a hub for cargo ships and also offers passenger services to neighboring countries such as Greece, Turkey, and Israel. The port of Larnaca also offers passenger services to other Mediterranean countries such as Egypt and Lebanon.

In terms of the quality of transportation in Cyprus, it is generally considered to be good. The road network is well-maintained, and there are plenty of options for getting around, including renting a car, using public transportation, cycling, or walking. The buses in Cyprus are modern, air-conditioned, and equipped with Wi-Fi, making them a convenient and affordable way to travel.

The airports in Cyprus are also modern and well-equipped, with facilities such as duty-free shops, restaurants, and car rental agencies. The national carrier, Cyprus Airways, offers both domestic and international flights, making it easy to travel to and from the island.

The ports in Cyprus are also well-equipped and offer passenger services to neighboring countries. The Port of Limassol is the largest port on the island and serves as a hub for cargo ships. It also offers passenger services to neighboring countries such as Greece, Turkey, and Israel. The port of Larnaca offers passenger services to other Mediterranean countries such as Egypt and Lebanon.

One potential issue with transportation in Cyprus is that it can become congested during peak tourist season, especially in popular tourist areas such as Limassol and Paphos. However, efforts have been made to improve traffic flow in these areas, such as the construction of new highways and the introduction of new public transportation routes.

Accommodation Options

Cyprus has a variety of accommodation options ranging from luxury resorts to budget-friendly hostels. In this article, we will explore the various accommodation options available in

Cyprus, their prices, and how to book them.

Hotels: Cyprus has a wide range of hotels ranging from budget-friendly to luxury options. Prices vary depending on the location and the amenities offered. Some popular hotel chains in Cyprus include Hilton, Radisson Blu, and Four Seasons. The average price for a standard double room in a mid-range hotel is around €70-€120 per night. For a luxury hotel, the price can go up to €300 or more per night.

Villas: If you are looking for a more private and spacious accommodation option, then renting a villa in Cyprus is a great option. Villas usually come with a private pool, fully equipped kitchen, and multiple bedrooms, making them perfect for families or groups of friends. The average price for a 3-bedroom villa with a private pool is around €150-€300 per night.

Apartments: Apartments are a popular accommodation option in Cyprus, especially for long-term stays. They come in a range of sizes and prices, making them suitable for solo travelers, couples, and families. The average price for a one-bedroom apartment in a central location is around €40-€80 per night.

Hostels: Hostels are a great option for budget-conscious travelers who want to meet other travelers and explore Cyprus. Hostels offer shared dorm rooms or private rooms at affordable prices. The average price for a bed in a dorm room is around €15-€30 per night.

Airbnb: Airbnb is a popular option for travelers who want to stay in a local home and experience the culture of Cyprus. Airbnb offers a wide range of accommodation options ranging from private rooms to entire apartments or villas. Prices vary depending on the location and amenities offered, but the average price for a one-bedroom apartment is around €50-€100 per night.

To book accommodation in Cyprus, there are several options available. You can book directly with the hotel, villa, or apartment owner through their website or by phone. Another option is to use online booking platforms such as Booking.com, Expedia, or Airbnb. These platforms allow you to compare prices, read reviews from other travelers, and book your accommodation directly.

In addition to considering your budget, location, and amenities, it is also important to consider the time of year you will be visiting Cyprus. Prices can vary greatly depending on the season, with peak season (June-September) being the most expensive. It is advisable to book your accommodation well in advance, especially during peak season, to ensure availability and the best prices.

When booking accommodation, be sure to read reviews from other travelers to get an idea of the quality of the accommodation and the level of service provided. Reviews can also provide valuable information about the location, amenities, and nearby attractions.

If you are planning to rent a villa or apartment, be sure to check the terms and conditions of the rental agreement carefully. Some owners may require a security deposit or have specific check-in and check-out times. It is also important to clarify the cleaning and maintenance responsibilities before booking.

When booking accommodation in Cyprus, it is important to keep in mind the local culture and customs. Cyprus is a conservative country, and it is important to respect local customs, especially when it comes to dress code and behavior in public areas. If you are unsure about local customs, it is advisable to do some research before your trip or ask your accommodation provider for advice.

Here are some examples of budget-friendly accommodation options in Cyprus, their prices, and locations:

Cyprus Hostels: Cyprus Hostels is a popular hostel chain with locations in Ayia Napa, Limassol, and Nicosia. The hostels offer shared dorm rooms and private rooms at affordable prices. Prices for a bed in a dorm room start at around €15 per night, while private rooms start at around €35 per night.

Napa Prince Hotel Apartments: Located in the heart of Ayia Napa, Napa Prince Hotel Apartments offers spacious and comfortable apartments at affordable prices. Prices for a one-bedroom apartment start at around €40 per night, while a two-bedroom apartment starts at around €60 per night.

Vrissaki Beach Hotel: Vrissaki Beach Hotel is located in the popular resort town of Protaras and offers affordable rooms and apartments just a short walk from the beach. Prices for a standard double room start at around €50 per night, while a one-bedroom apartment starts at around €60 per night.

Evkarpos Country House: Evkarpos Country House is located in the picturesque village of Lofou and offers affordable accommodation in a traditional Cypriot setting. Prices for a double room start at around €50 per night, while a family room starts at around €70 per night.

Charalambos Holiday Cottage: Charalambos Holiday Cottage is located in the village of Vavla and offers affordable self-catering accommodation in a traditional Cypriot cottage. Prices for a one-bedroom cottage start at around €50 per night, while a two-bedroom cottage starts at around €70 per night.

Oinoessa Traditional Boutique Guest Houses: Located in the picturesque village of Lofou, Oinoessa Traditional Boutique Guest Houses offers affordable accommodation in beautifully restored traditional Cypriot houses. Prices for a double room start at around €70 per night, while a one-bedroom suite starts at around €110 per night.

Paphos Inn Hostel: Located in the historic center of Paphos, Paphos Inn Hostel offers budget-friendly dorm rooms and private rooms with shared bathrooms. Prices for a bed in a dorm room start at around €15 per night, while a private double room starts at around €30 per night.

Tala Amphora Hotel Apartments: Tala Amphora Hotel Apartments is located in the village of Tala, just a short drive from Paphos town and the beach. The apartments offer affordable self-catering accommodation with a pool and a restaurant on-site. Prices for a studio apartment start at around €45 per night, while a one-bedroom apartment starts at around €65 per night.

Hotel Opera: Located in the heart of Nicosia, Hotel Opera offers affordable rooms and suites in a convenient location. Prices for a standard double room start at around €60 per night, while a suite starts at around €90 per night.

Island Boutique Hotel: Located in the popular resort town of Ayia Napa, Island Boutique Hotel offers affordable rooms and suites just a short walk from the beach. Prices for a standard double room start at around €70 per night, while a suite starts at around €110 per night.

There are plenty of budget-friendly accommodation options in Cyprus that offer comfortable and convenient places to stay without breaking the bank. When booking budget-friendly accommodation, it's important to do your research and read reviews to ensure that the property meets your needs and expectations.

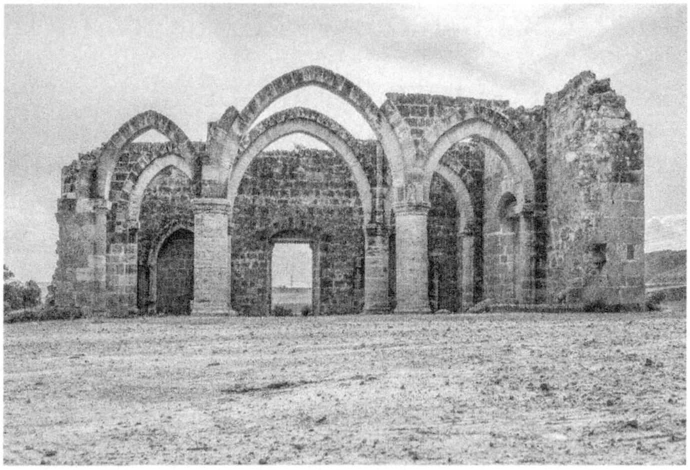

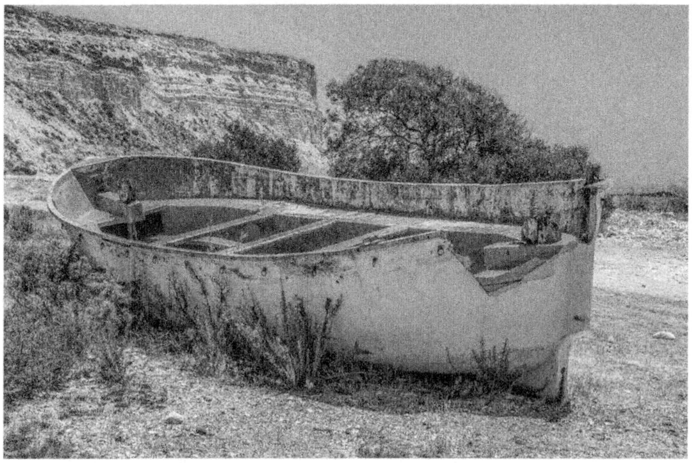

Chapter 3: Top Destinations in Cyprus

Nicosia

Nicosia, also known as Lefkosia, is the capital city of the island of Cyprus. It is situated in the heart of the island and is the largest city in Cyprus, with a population of over 300,000 people. Nicosia is known for its rich history, vibrant culture, and diverse architecture.

Nicosia is a city that has been inhabited for over 4,500 years. It was founded by the Greeks in the 4th century BC and has since been ruled by various empires, including the Romans, the Byzantines, the Venetians, the Ottomans, and the British. As a result, the city has a rich cultural heritage and boasts a unique blend of architectural styles, including Gothic, Renaissance, and Ottoman.

One of the most prominent landmarks in Nicosia is the Venetian walls that surround the city. These walls were built in the 16th century by the Venetians to protect the city from invaders. The walls are well-preserved and are a testament to the city's long history.

Another significant landmark in Nicosia is the Selimiye Mosque, which was originally built as the Cathedral of Saint Sophia during the Lusignan period in the 13th century. The building was converted into a mosque during the Ottoman period and is now a UNESCO World Heritage Site. It is an impressive example of Gothic and Ottoman architecture.

The old town of Nicosia is another must-see attraction. It is a maze of narrow streets, alleys, and squares that are home to traditional Cypriot houses, shops, and restaurants. The old town is also home to several museums, including the Cyprus Museum, which houses an extensive collection of archaeological artifacts from the island's prehistoric and medieval periods.

One of the most unique features of Nicosia is the Green Line, which is a buffer zone that separates the northern and southern parts of the city. The Green Line was established in 1964 after inter-communal violence between the Greek Cypriots and Turkish Cypriots. Today, the Green Line is a reminder of the island's turbulent past and is a symbol of the ongoing division between the two communities.

Nicosia is also a city that is full of life and energy. The city center is a hub of activity, with a variety of shops, cafes, and restaurants. The city also hosts several cultural events throughout the year, including the Nicosia International Film Festival and the Cyprus International Festival.

Top Attractions

Nicosia is a city with a rich history and culture, which is reflected in its numerous attractions. Here are some of the must-see attractions in Nicosia:

Venetian Walls: The Venetian Walls were built in the 16th century to protect the city from invaders. The walls are well-preserved and offer stunning views of the city.

Selimiye Mosque: Originally built as the Cathedral of Saint Sophia during the Lusignan period in the 13th century, the Selimiye Mosque is an impressive example of Gothic and Ottoman architecture.

The Cyprus Museum: The Cyprus Museum is the oldest and largest archaeological museum in Cyprus. It houses an extensive collection of artifacts from the island's prehistoric and medieval periods.

Ledra Street: Ledra Street is the main shopping street in Nicosia. It is a pedestrian-only zone and is home to a variety of shops, cafes, and restaurants.

Faneromeni Square: Faneromeni Square is a popular meeting spot in Nicosia. It is home to the Church of Faneromeni, which is a significant religious site in the city.

Laiki Geitonia: Laiki Geitonia is a traditional neighborhood in Nicosia. It is a maze of narrow streets and alleys that are home to traditional Cypriot houses, shops, and restaurants.

The Famagusta Gate: The Famagusta Gate is one of the three gates in the Venetian Walls. It was built in the 16th century and is now a cultural center that hosts various exhibitions and events.

The Cyprus Folk Art Museum: The Cyprus Folk Art Museum is located in a traditional house in the old town of Nicosia. It houses a collection of traditional Cypriot crafts, including pottery, weaving, and lace-making.

St. John's Cathedral: St. John's Cathedral is a Catholic cathedral in Nicosia. It was built in the 17th century and is a beautiful example of Baroque architecture.

The Dervish Pasha Mansion: The Dervish Pasha Mansion is a traditional Ottoman mansion that has been converted into a museum. It houses an exhibition on the history and culture of Nicosia.

Where to Eat

Nicosia is a city with a vibrant food scene, with a variety of options to suit all tastes and budgets. Here are some of the best places to eat in Nicosia:

To Kafe Tis Chrysanthi's: This is a popular coffee shop in the old town of

Nicosia. It serves traditional Cypriot coffee and pastries, such as bougatsa and loukoumades.

Kantina: This is a casual restaurant that serves traditional Cypriot food, including souvlaki, kebab, and grilled halloumi. The portions are generous, and the prices are reasonable.

Epsilon Resto Bar: This is a trendy restaurant and bar that serves Mediterranean-inspired cuisine. The menu includes a variety of meze dishes, grilled meats, and seafood.

Valtou Rigani: This is a cozy restaurant in the old town of Nicosia. It serves traditional Cypriot food, including kleftiko, moussaka, and stifado. The portions are generous, and the prices are reasonable.

Piatsa Gourounaki: This is a casual restaurant that serves grilled meats and traditional Cypriot dishes. The portions are generous, and the prices are reasonable.

Fat Chef: This is a popular restaurant that serves Mediterranean-inspired cuisine. The menu includes a variety of dishes, including pasta, risotto, and grilled meats.

Berengaria Cafe: This is a charming cafe in the old town of Nicosia. It serves traditional Cypriot coffee and pastries, such as bougatsa and koulouri.

Kipros Souvlaki: This is a casual restaurant that serves traditional Cypriot souvlaki. The portions are generous, and the prices are reasonable.

The Gym: This is a trendy restaurant and bar that serves international cuisine. The menu includes a variety of dishes, including burgers, sushi, and salads.

To Brunch: This is a cozy cafe that serves breakfast and brunch dishes, including pancakes, eggs benedict, and avocado toast.

Nightlife

Nicosia is a city with a lively nightlife, offering a range of options for those looking to have a good time. Here are some of the best places to enjoy the nightlife in Nicosia:

Loft Club: This is a popular nightclub located in the city center. It features a spacious dance floor, high-quality sound system, and a variety of DJs playing a mix of electronic, house, and techno music.

Guaba Beach Bar: This is a beach-themed bar that features a dance floor, a swimming pool, and a stage for live music and DJs. It's a great spot to enjoy a drink and dance the night away.

Black and White: This is a popular nightclub that features a spacious dance floor, VIP area, and a variety of DJs playing a mix of electronic, house, and R&B music.

7 Seas: This is a stylish rooftop bar located on top of a hotel. It features stunning views of the city, a variety of cocktails, and live music events.

Kafeneio: This is a popular bar in the old town of Nicosia. It features live music events, a variety of cocktails, and a cozy atmosphere.

Silver Star: This is a popular nightclub that features a spacious dance floor, a VIP area, and a variety of DJs playing a mix of electronic, house, and R&B music.

Shakespeare Pub: This is a cozy pub in the old town of Nicosia. It features a variety of beers, cocktails, and live music events.

Zanettos: This is a popular cafe in the old town of Nicosia that turns into a lively bar at night. It features a variety of cocktails, beers, and live music events.

Aperitivo Jazz Bar: This is a cozy jazz bar that features live music events, a variety of cocktails, and a relaxing atmosphere.

Havana Social: This is a trendy cocktail bar that features a variety of signature cocktails, a Cuban-themed atmosphere, and live music events.

It's worth noting that Nicosia's nightlife scene caters to a diverse crowd, with options for those who prefer a laid-back evening as well as those who want to party until the early hours of the morning. Many of the bars and clubs are located in the city center, making it easy to hop from one spot to another.

Additionally, Nicosia is known for its street parties and festivals throughout the year, such as the Nicosia Carnival, the Nicosia Beer Festival, and the Nicosia Jazz Festival. These events attract both locals and visitors alike and offer a great opportunity to experience the city's vibrant and diverse cultural scene.

For those who prefer a more low-key evening, there are plenty of options for enjoying a relaxed drink or meal with friends. The city is dotted with cozy cafes, wine bars, and traditional tavernas that offer a more laid-back atmosphere.

Day Trip from Nicosia

Nicosia is a city full of history and culture, but it's also surrounded by beautiful landscapes and attractions that are well worth a day trip. Here are some of the top day trip destinations from Nicosia:

Troodos Mountains: Located about an hour's drive from Nicosia, the Troodos Mountains offer stunning scenery and plenty of outdoor activities. Hiking trails, picturesque villages, and ancient churches are just a few of the things to explore in this scenic region.

Larnaca: Located about 40 minutes from Nicosia, the coastal town of Larnaca is a popular day trip destination for those looking to enjoy the sea and sun. Larnaca's beaches are some of the best in Cyprus, and the town also boasts a lively promenade, museums, and historic sites.

Limassol: This bustling seaside city is located about an hour's drive from Nicosia and offers plenty of attractions for a day trip. From its scenic marina to its historic old town, Limassol is a great place to explore for those interested in history, culture, and seaside fun.

Paphos: Located about two hours from Nicosia, the coastal city of Paphos is a UNESCO World Heritage Site and offers a wealth of ancient ruins, including the famous Tomb of the Kings and the Paphos Archaeological Park. It's also home to beautiful beaches, a charming harbor, and a picturesque old town.

Nicosia Buffer Zone: For a unique day trip experience, consider exploring the Nicosia Buffer Zone, which divides the city between the Greek Cypriot and Turkish Cypriot communities. The buffer zone is a fascinating and poignant reminder of the island's complex history and offers plenty of historic sites, museums, and cultural experiences.

Where to Relax and Enjoy

Nicosia is a city that offers plenty of opportunities to relax and enjoy some downtime. Here are some of the top spots to unwind in and around the city:

Public parks: Nicosia is home to several beautiful parks, including the Municipal Gardens and the Acropolis Park. These parks offer a peaceful oasis in the heart of the city, with plenty of green space, walking paths, and benches to relax on.

Hammam Omerye: This traditional Turkish bathhouse is located in the heart of Nicosia's old town and offers a range of spa treatments and massages to help you unwind and de-stress. The beautiful, historic building and tranquil atmosphere make it the perfect place to escape from the hustle and bustle of the city.

Zenon Spa: Located in the Hilton Cyprus hotel, Zenon Spa offers a range of spa treatments, including massages, facials, and body treatments. The spa also features a sauna, steam room, and indoor pool, making it a great place to relax and rejuvenate.

Larnaca Salt Lake: Located about 40 minutes from Nicosia, the Larnaca Salt Lake is a beautiful spot to enjoy nature and soak up some sun. The lake is surrounded by a nature trail and is home to a variety of bird species, making it a popular spot for birdwatching.

Beaches: While Nicosia is an inland city, there are several beautiful beaches within an hour's drive of the city. Popular options include Mackenzie

Beach in Larnaca and Finikoudes Beach in Ayia Napa. Both beaches offer soft sand, clear water, and plenty of beachside restaurants and cafes.

Ayia Napa Sculpture Park: Located about an hour's drive from Nicosia, the Ayia Napa Sculpture Park is a unique outdoor art gallery featuring sculptures by artists from around the world. The park is located near the beach and offers a peaceful and serene atmosphere to enjoy some art and nature.

St. George's Beach: This beach is located in the Paphos area, about two hours from Nicosia. It's a quieter option than some of the more popular beaches, and its crystal-clear water and scenic views make it a great spot to relax and unwind.

Aphrodite's Rock: This iconic rock formation is located about an hour and a half from Nicosia and is said to be the birthplace of the goddess Aphrodite. The rock is a popular spot for photos and offers stunning views of the sea and surrounding landscape.

Traditional villages: Cyprus is home to many charming traditional villages that offer a glimpse into the island's rich history and culture. Some of the top villages to visit include Lefkara, known for its lace-making tradition, and Omodos, known for its wineries and historic monastery.

Spa resorts: If you're looking for the ultimate relaxation experience, consider staying at one of Cyprus's many spa resorts. These resorts offer a range of luxurious amenities, including pools, hot tubs, saunas, and spa treatments, making them the perfect place to unwind and enjoy some pampering.

Limassol

Limassol is a coastal city located in southern Cyprus, an island country in the eastern Mediterranean Sea. It is the second-largest city in Cyprus, with a population of over 240,000 residents, and is known for its beautiful beaches, historic landmarks, and vibrant nightlife. In this article, we will provide a comprehensive overview of Limassol, including its history, culture, economy, and tourism.

History: Limassol has a rich history that dates back to ancient times. It was originally known as Nea Salamis, a Greek colony that was founded in the 12th century BC. Over the centuries, the city was ruled by various powers, including the Persians, Romans, and Byzantines. In the 16th century, Limassol was occupied by the Ottomans, who controlled the city until it was ceded to the British in 1878. After Cyprus gained independence in 1960, Limassol continued to grow and develop, becoming one of the island's major cities.

Culture: Limassol is a cosmopolitan city that reflects the diverse cultures and traditions of its residents. The city is home to a variety of museums, galleries, and cultural institutions, including the Limassol Archaeological Museum, the Limassol Municipal Art Gallery, and the Cyprus Wine Museum. Traditional festivals and events are also an important part of Limassol's culture, with celebrations such as Carnival, the Limassol Wine Festival, and the Limassol Beer Festival drawing crowds of locals and tourists each year.

Economy: Limassol is a major economic center in Cyprus, with a thriving service sector that includes banking, finance, and shipping. The city's port is one of the busiest in the

Mediterranean, and Limassol is also home to many international companies and organizations. The Limassol Marina, a luxury residential and commercial development, has become a popular destination for both locals and tourists, with high-end shops, restaurants, and apartments.

Tourism: Tourism is a significant industry in Limassol, with the city attracting millions of visitors each year. The city's beautiful beaches, clear blue waters, and warm climate make it a popular destination for sun-seekers and water sports enthusiasts. Limassol is also known for its historical and cultural landmarks, including the Limassol Castle, the Kourion Archaeological Site, and the ancient city of Amathus. The city's vibrant nightlife scene, with its bars, clubs, and restaurants, is also a major draw for tourists.

Limassol is a fascinating and diverse city that offers something for everyone. With its rich history, vibrant culture, strong economy, and stunning natural beauty, it is no wonder that Limassol is one of the most popular destinations in Cyprus.

Top attractions

Limassol is a coastal city in Cyprus that offers many exciting attractions for tourists to explore. Whether you're interested in history, culture, or simply enjoying the beautiful beaches and scenery, Limassol has something to offer. Here are some of the top attractions in Limassol that you won't want to miss:

Limassol Castle: Located in the heart of the old town, Limassol Castle is a must-visit attraction for history buffs. Originally built in the 13th century by the Byzantines, the castle was later modified and expanded by the

Lusignans, Venetians, and Ottomans. Today, it houses the Cyprus Medieval Museum, which showcases the island's rich history from the 3rd century AD to the end of the Ottoman period.

Kourion Archaeological Site: Located about 19 kilometers west of Limassol, the Kourion Archaeological Site is a fascinating historical attraction that dates back to the Roman period. The site features an ancient amphitheater, Roman baths, and a mosaic-filled House of Eustolios. Visitors can also enjoy stunning views of the surrounding coastline and countryside.

Limassol Marina: The Limassol Marina is a modern development that has quickly become one of the city's top attractions. Featuring a luxury yacht marina, high-end shops, restaurants, and apartments, the marina offers visitors a chance to indulge in some upscale retail therapy and waterfront dining.

Old Town: The old town of Limassol is a charming area filled with narrow streets, colorful buildings, and traditional architecture. It is the perfect place to wander and explore, with plenty of shops, cafes, and historical landmarks to discover. Be sure to visit the Agios Andreas Church and the Ayia

Napa Church, both of which date back to the 16th century.

Limassol Zoo: Located in the heart of the city, the Limassol Zoo is a fun family-friendly attraction that is home to over 300 animals from around the world. Visitors can see lions, tigers, bears, monkeys, and many other animals in naturalistic habitats.

Municipal Gardens: The Municipal Gardens in Limassol are a tranquil oasis in the heart of the city. Featuring lush greenery, fountains, and shaded seating areas, the gardens are the perfect place to relax and escape the hustle and bustle of the city.

Amathus Archaeological Site: Located just outside of Limassol, the Amathus Archaeological Site is a fascinating historical attraction that dates back to the 7th century BC. The site features the remains of an ancient city that was once a major center of trade and commerce in the Mediterranean. Visitors can explore the ruins of temples, palaces, and public buildings, as well as the city's impressive defensive walls.

Limassol Sculpture Park: The Limassol Sculpture Park is a unique and creative attraction that features a collection of contemporary sculptures from local and international artists. The park covers an area of over 20,000 square meters and is situated in the Molos area of Limassol, near the seafront.

Wine Tasting Tours: Cyprus is known for its delicious wines, and Limassol is a great place to indulge in some wine tasting. The city is surrounded by vineyards, and there are several wineries in the area that offer tours and tastings. Some of the top wineries to visit include the Vouni Panayia Winery, the Ayia Mavri Winery, and the Kolossi Castle Winery.

Limassol Municipal Art Gallery: The Limassol Municipal Art Gallery is a great place to explore the local art scene. The gallery features a collection of works by contemporary Cypriot artists, as well as temporary exhibitions of international artists. The gallery is located in the old town of Limassol and is housed in a beautiful old building.

Fasouri Watermania Water Park: For families with kids, the Fasouri Watermania Water Park is a must-visit attraction. Located just outside of Limassol, the water park features a variety of water slides, pools, and attractions, as well as restaurants and snack bars.

Where to Eat

Limassol is known for its delicious cuisine, which is a fusion of Mediterranean and Middle Eastern flavors. From traditional tavernas and meze restaurants to trendy cafes and fine dining establishments, there is no shortage of great places to eat in Limassol. Here are some of the top places to eat in the city:

To Ouzeri: To Ouzeri is a traditional meze restaurant that offers a wide variety of small dishes that are perfect for sharing. The menu features local specialties like grilled halloumi cheese, stuffed grape leaves, and lamb souvlaki, as well as fresh seafood dishes. The restaurant is located in the old town of Limassol and has a cozy and relaxed atmosphere.

Kanika Fish Tavern: Kanika Fish Tavern is a seafood restaurant that is located right on the beachfront in Limassol. The menu features a variety of fresh fish and seafood dishes, including grilled octopus, fried calamari, and sea bass. The restaurant has a great atmosphere and is perfect for a romantic dinner or a night out with friends.

Vinylio Wine Bar and Bistro: Vinylio Wine Bar and Bistro is a trendy restaurant that offers a fusion of Mediterranean and international cuisine. The menu features dishes like lamb chops, grilled octopus, and beetroot salad, as well as a great selection of wines from around the world. The restaurant is located in the old town of Limassol and has a cool and contemporary atmosphere.

Kalamies: Kalamies is a traditional Cypriot restaurant that is located in the village of Parekklisia, just outside of Limassol. The menu features dishes like kleftiko (slow-roasted lamb), moussaka, and pastitsio, as well as meze platters that are perfect for sharing. The restaurant has a rustic and charming atmosphere, with outdoor seating surrounded by olive trees.

Artima Bistro: Artima Bistro is a chic and stylish restaurant that offers a fusion of Mediterranean and international cuisine. The menu features dishes like steak with truffle butter, sea bass with fennel and orange, and risotto with wild mushrooms. The restaurant is located in the Limassol Marina and has a beautiful waterfront setting.

The Tea Room: The Tea Room is a quaint and cozy cafe that offers a variety of teas, coffees, and light bites. The menu features homemade cakes and pastries, as well as sandwiches and salads. The cafe is located in the old town of Limassol and has a relaxed and welcoming atmosphere.

Puesta Oyster Bar and Grill: Puesta Oyster Bar and Grill is a seafood restaurant that offers a range of fresh fish and seafood dishes, as well as grilled meats and vegetarian options. The menu features dishes like oysters, sushi, grilled octopus, and lobster, as well as a variety of cocktails and wines.

The restaurant is located in the Limassol Marina and has a modern and stylish atmosphere.

Militzis Traditional Restaurant: Militzis Traditional Restaurant is a family-run restaurant that offers authentic Cypriot cuisine. The menu features dishes like grilled halloumi cheese, kleftiko, and stuffed vegetables, as well as a variety of meze platters. The restaurant has a warm and welcoming atmosphere and is located in the old town of Limassol.

La Boca: La Boca is a steakhouse that offers a range of grilled meats, including wagyu beef and angus beef.

The menu also features a variety of salads and side dishes, as well as a great selection of wines. The restaurant is located in the Limassol Marina and has a contemporary and sophisticated atmosphere.

Souvlaki Bar: Souvlaki Bar is a casual eatery that offers traditional Greek and Cypriot souvlaki. The menu features a variety of meats, including pork, chicken, and lamb, as well as vegetarian options like grilled halloumi cheese. The restaurant has a laid-back atmosphere and is perfect for a quick and tasty lunch.

Artisan's Burgerbar: Artisan's Burgerbar is a trendy restaurant that offers a range of gourmet burgers made with fresh and locally-sourced ingredients. The menu features burgers like the Classic Cheeseburger, the Greek Burger, and the Truffle Burger, as well as salads and sides. The restaurant is located in the Limassol Marina and has a cool and contemporary atmosphere.

Nightlife

Limassol is one of the liveliest cities in Cyprus, famous for its beautiful beaches, rich culture, and vibrant nightlife. The city boasts of an eclectic mix of bars, pubs, clubs, and entertainment venues that cater to the tastes of locals and tourists alike. In this article, we will explore the various aspects of Limassol's nightlife and what makes it so special.

Bars and Pubs: Limassol is home to a plethora of bars and pubs, offering a relaxed and chilled-out atmosphere for those who want to unwind after a long day. Whether you are looking for a trendy cocktail bar, a cozy pub, or a beach bar with stunning views, you will find it all in Limassol. Some of the popular bars and pubs in the city include The Library Bar, The Gin

Garden, The Woodman Sports Pub & Restaurant, and the Wine & More Bar.

The Library Bar is located in the heart of Limassol's old town and offers a sophisticated atmosphere with a wide selection of premium spirits, cocktails, and wines. The Gin Garden, on the other hand, is a trendy bar that specializes in gin-based cocktails and offers a beautiful outdoor seating area with stunning views of the sea. The Woodman Sports Pub & Restaurant is a popular haunt among sports enthusiasts and offers a wide selection of beers, wines, and spirits along with delicious pub food. The Wine & More

Bar, as the name suggests, is a wine bar that offers an extensive selection of local and international wines, along with delicious tapas.

Clubs and Nightlife Venues: If you are looking for a more upbeat and lively atmosphere, Limassol has plenty of clubs and nightlife venues to choose from. The city has a vibrant club scene, with some of the best DJs in the world performing at various venues. Some of the popular clubs and nightlife venues in Limassol include Guaba Beach Bar, Breeze Summer Club, Base Club, and the Monte Caputo Club.

Guaba Beach Bar is a world-renowned beach club that has been ranked among the best clubs in the world. It hosts some of the biggest parties in Cyprus and attracts thousands of party-goers every year. Breeze Summer Club is another popular beach club that offers a stunning setting with breathtaking views of the sea. Base Club is a stylish nightclub that features state-of-the-art sound and lighting systems, while Monte Caputo Club is a popular venue for live music, concerts, and performances.

Events and Festivals: In addition to its bars, pubs, and clubs, Limassol also hosts a variety of events and festivals throughout the year. These events showcase the best of Limassol's cultural and artistic offerings and are a great way to experience the city's nightlife. Some of the popular events and festivals in Limassol include the Limassol Wine Festival, the Carnival Parade, and the Limassol Beer Festival.

The Limassol Wine Festival is a must-visit event for wine lovers, as it offers the opportunity to sample some of the best wines from the region. The Carnival Parade is a colorful and vibrant event that takes place before Lent and features parades, music, and dance performances. The Limassol Beer

Festival, as the name suggests, is a celebration of beer and features live music, food, and, of course, plenty of beer.

Limassol's nightlife is one of the best in Cyprus and offers something for everyone. Whether you are looking for a relaxed evening at a cozy pub or a wild night out at a nightclub, Limassol has it all. The city's vibrant club scene, stunning beach bars, and cultural events make it a popular destination for party-goers and tourists alike. So, if you're planning a trip to Cyprus, make sure to

Day trip from Limassol

Limassol, a bustling coastal city located in the southern part of Cyprus, offers a lot of opportunities for travelers to explore the surrounding areas. With its excellent transport links and central location, Limassol serves as an ideal base to explore the island's many attractions. Here, we will explore some of the best day trips from Limassol.

Kourion and Kolossi Castle: One of the most popular day trips from Limassol is a visit to the ancient city of Kourion and the nearby Kolossi Castle. Kourion is a well-preserved Greco-Roman archaeological site that offers a glimpse into Cyprus's rich history. The site includes a well-preserved amphitheater, a Roman house, and a public bath complex. Kolossi Castle, located a few kilometers away, is a medieval castle built in the 13th century by the Knights of Saint John. The castle offers stunning views of the surrounding area and is a must-visit for history buffs.

Troodos Mountains: The Troodos Mountains, located in the central part of Cyprus, offer a picturesque landscape of rugged peaks, rolling hills, and scenic villages. The mountains are home to several hiking trails, including the Caledonia Waterfalls Trail and the Artemis Trail, both of which offer stunning views of the countryside. The Troodos Mountains are also home to several traditional mountain villages, including Omodos, which is famous for its wine, and Kakopetria, which is renowned for its picturesque cobbled streets and traditional architecture.

Paphos: Paphos, located on the western coast of Cyprus, is a popular day trip destination from Limassol. The city is home to several ancient monuments, including the Tombs of the Kings, a UNESCO World Heritage Site, and the

Paphos Archaeological Park, which includes well-preserved mosaics and ruins. Paphos is also home to several beautiful beaches, including Coral Bay and Lara Bay, which is a protected area for nesting sea turtles.

Nicosia: Nicosia, the capital city of Cyprus, is a bustling metropolis located in the center of the island. The city is known for its rich history, cultural heritage, and stunning architecture. Visitors can explore the city's many museums, including the Cyprus Museum, which houses artifacts from the island's ancient past, and the Leventis Municipal Museum, which showcases the city's history and culture. Nicosia is also home to several stunning landmarks, including the Venetian Walls and the Selimiye Mosque, which was once a Gothic cathedral.

Akamas Peninsula: The Akamas Peninsula, located on the western tip of Cyprus, is a protected area of natural beauty that offers stunning scenery, pristine beaches, and rugged terrain. The area is home to several hiking trails, including the Aphrodite Trail, which leads to the mythical birthplace of the goddess of love. Visitors can also explore the peninsula's many beaches, including Lara Beach, which is a protected nesting site for loggerhead sea turtles.

Limassol serves as an ideal base to explore the many attractions that Cyprus has to offer. From ancient archaeological sites and medieval castles to picturesque mountain villages and stunning natural landscapes, there is something for everyone. So, if you're planning a trip to Cyprus, make sure to set aside some time to explore the surrounding areas of Limassol.

Where Relax and Enjoy

Limassol is a popular tourist destination on the southern coast of Cyprus that offers a wide range of options for visitors to relax and enjoy their vacation. From beaches and parks to spas and wellness centers, here are some of the top places where visitors can unwind and enjoy their time in Limassol.

Beaches: Limassol is known for its beautiful beaches, which offer visitors a chance to soak up the sun and enjoy the Mediterranean Sea. Some of the most popular beaches in Limassol include

Dasoudi Beach, Lady's Mile Beach, and Curium Beach. These beaches are open to the public and free of charge, although visitors will need to pay for sun loungers and umbrellas if they want to use them.

Parks: Limassol has several parks that offer a peaceful escape from the hustle and bustle of the city. One of the most popular parks is the Municipal Gardens, which features a variety of trees, flowers, and a small zoo. The park is free to enter and is open from 6:30 am until late in the evening.

Spas and Wellness Centers: For those looking to pamper themselves,

Limassol has several spas and wellness centers that offer a range of treatments and services. One of the most popular is the Anagenesis Spa at the Four Seasons Hotel, which offers a variety of massages, facials, and body treatments. Prices for treatments start at around €80 ($95) for a 60-minute massage.

Waterparks: Families with children may enjoy spending a day at one of the waterparks in Limassol. The most popular waterpark is Fasouri Watermania, which features several water slides, a lazy river, and a wave pool. Tickets start at around €30 ($35) for adults and €17 ($20) for children.

Restaurants and Bars: Limassol has a vibrant dining and nightlife scene, with a range of restaurants and bars to suit all tastes and budgets. Visitors can enjoy a meal at a traditional Cypriot taverna or try international cuisine at one of the city's many restaurants. Prices vary depending on the establishment, but visitors can expect to pay around €20-30 ($24-$35) per person for a meal at a mid-range restaurant.

Limassol Marina: For those looking to relax by the water, Limassol Marina is a beautiful place to spend an afternoon. The marina is home to several cafes and restaurants, as well as a variety of luxury shops and boutiques. Visitors can enjoy a meal with a view of the yachts or take a stroll along the waterfront. Prices at the restaurants and cafes vary, but visitors can expect to pay around €15-25 ($18-$30) per person for a meal.

Wine Tasting: Cyprus is known for its wine, and Limassol is home to several wineries that offer wine tastings and tours. One of the most popular is the Keo Winery, which offers daily tours and tastings for €8 ($9.50) per person. Visitors can sample a range of wines and learn about the history and production process of Cypriot wine.

Cultural Sites: For those interested in history and culture, Limassol has several sites that are worth a visit. The Limassol Castle, which dates back to the 14th century, houses the Cyprus Medieval Museum and offers a glimpse into the island's past. Tickets are €4.50 ($5.30) for adults and €2.50 ($3) for children. The Kolossi Castle, located just outside of Limassol, is another popular cultural site. Tickets are €2.50 ($3) for adults and €1.25 ($1.50) for children.

Golf Courses: Limassol is home to several golf courses, including the Aphrodite Hills Golf Club and the Secret Valley Golf Club. These courses offer visitors a chance to relax and enjoy a round of golf in a beautiful setting. Prices vary depending on the course and time of year, but visitors can expect to pay around €70-100 ($83-$118) per round.

Hiking and Nature Trails: For those looking to explore the natural beauty of Limassol, there are several hiking and nature trails to choose from. The Akamas Peninsula, located just outside of Limassol, offers several trails that wind through the rugged landscape and offer stunning views of the Mediterranean Sea. The Limassol Forest, located in the Troodos

Mountains, is another popular spot for hiking and nature walks. These trails are free to access, but visitors should be prepared for rugged terrain and bring plenty of water.

Paphos

Paphos is a coastal city situated in the southwestern region of the Mediterranean island of Cyprus. It is a popular tourist destination known for its rich history, natural beauty, and mild climate. Paphos was designated as the European Capital of Culture in 2017, which has further boosted its popularity among tourists.

The city of Paphos is divided into two distinct areas: the coastal region and the inland area. The coastal region is where most of the tourist activities take place. It is dotted with several beautiful beaches, including Coral Bay, which is one of the most popular beaches on the island. The region is also home to several luxury resorts, restaurants, bars, and cafes, which cater to the needs of tourists.

The inland area of Paphos is where the city's historical and cultural attractions are located. It is home to the famous archaeological site of Kato Paphos, which has been designated as a UNESCO World Heritage Site. The site features several ancient ruins, including the Temple of Aphrodite, the Roman Odeon, and the House of Dionysus. The Tombs of the Kings is another popular historical site, which features underground tombs carved out of solid rock.

Paphos is also famous for its natural beauty. The region is dotted with several parks and gardens, including the Paphos Municipal Park and the Paphos Aphrodite Water Park. The Akamas Peninsula, which is located near Paphos, is a nature reserve that features several hiking trails, beautiful beaches, and stunning landscapes.

The city of Paphos also boasts a vibrant nightlife. The main party hub is located in the coastal region, where several bars and nightclubs stay open until the early hours of the morning.

Paphos is a beautiful city that offers a perfect blend of history, culture, natural beauty, and modern amenities. Whether you are interested in exploring ancient ruins, relaxing on beautiful beaches, or partying the night away, Paphos has something to offer for everyone.

Top attractions

Paphos is a city rich in history, culture, and natural beauty, offering a plethora of attractions for visitors to explore.

Here are some of the top attractions in Paphos:

Kato Paphos Archaeological Park: The park is a UNESCO World Heritage site, located near the harbor in Paphos. It is one of the most significant archaeological sites in Cyprus, featuring ancient ruins that date back to the Roman and Byzantine periods. The park covers an area of around 15 hectares and includes the House of Dionysus, the House of Theseus, the Roman Odeon, and the Agora.

Tombs of the Kings: Located just outside Paphos, the Tombs of the Kings is a collection of underground tombs dating back to the Hellenistic and

Roman periods. The tombs are carved out of solid rock, featuring intricate designs and decorations. The site is known for its grandeur and size, which is why it was given its name.

Paphos Castle: This medieval fortress is situated on the harbor of Paphos and was built in the 13th century by the Lusignans. It has since been restored and is now used as a museum. The castle is a popular attraction due to its history and stunning views of the sea.

Aphrodite's Rock: This is a popular attraction located on the coast of Paphos. According to Greek mythology, this is where the goddess of love, Aphrodite, was born. The rock is located near Petra tou Romiou beach and is a popular spot for taking photos.

Akamas Peninsula: The Akamas Peninsula is a protected area of natural beauty, located in the northwestern region of Paphos. The area is known for its stunning landscapes, hiking trails, and beaches. Visitors can explore the area by foot, bike, or 4x4 vehicle.

Coral Bay: Coral Bay is one of the most popular beaches in Paphos, located in the western part of the city. It is known for its crystal clear waters, white sand,

and stunning sunsets. The beach is a popular spot for swimming, sunbathing, and water sports.

Paphos Aphrodite Water Park: This water park is located in the coastal region of Paphos and is a popular attraction for families. It features a range of water slides, pools, and attractions for visitors of all ages.

Paphos Municipal Park: This park is located in the heart of Paphos and is a popular spot for picnics, strolls, and relaxation. It features a range of facilities, including a playground, a small zoo, and a botanical garden.

Saint Neophytos Monastery: The monastery is located near Tala village, just outside Paphos. It was founded in the 12th century by Saint Neophytos and is known for its intricate frescoes and stunning views of the surrounding area.

Mosaics of Paphos: The Mosaics of Paphos are a collection of well-preserved Roman mosaics that date back to the 2nd century AD. They are located in the Kato Paphos Archaeological Park and feature intricate designs and depictions of Greek mythology.

Where to Eat

Paphos is a city that offers a diverse range of dining options, from traditional Cypriot cuisine to international dishes. Here are some of the best places to eat in Paphos:

Gabriel's Tavern: This traditional tavern is located in the heart of Paphos and offers a range of Cypriot dishes, including souvlaki, meze, and kleftiko. The restaurant has a relaxed atmosphere and is popular among both locals and tourists.

Muse: This restaurant is located near the harbor in Paphos and offers a range of international dishes, including seafood, sushi, and pasta. The restaurant has a modern and stylish atmosphere and is a popular spot for couples and groups.

Ta Piatakia: This taverna is located in the Kato Paphos area and offers a range of traditional Cypriot dishes, including grilled meats and meze. The restaurant has a rustic and cozy atmosphere and is a popular spot for families and groups.

Fat Mama's: This Italian restaurant is located in the Tomb of the Kings area and offers a range of pasta, pizza, and other Italian dishes. The restaurant has a fun and lively atmosphere and is popular among families and groups.

The Lodge Steak & Seafood Co: This restaurant is located in the Coral Bay area and offers a range of steaks, seafood, and other international dishes. The restaurant has a cozy and relaxed atmosphere and is popular among couples and groups.

Muse Café Kitchen Bar: This café is located in the heart of Paphos and offers a range of breakfast, lunch, and dinner options. The café has a modern and stylish atmosphere and is popular among locals and tourists.

Kyklos Greek Restaurant: This restaurant is located in the Kato Paphos area and offers a range of Greek dishes, including moussaka, souvlaki, and Greek salad. The restaurant has a traditional and cozy atmosphere and is popular among families and groups.

Pambis Diner: This restaurant is located in the Tomb of the Kings area and offers a range of international dishes, including burgers, pizza, and salads. The restaurant has a fun and casual atmosphere and is popular among families and groups.

Lighthouse Beach Bar & Restaurant: This restaurant is located near the lighthouse in Paphos and offers a range of seafood, salads, and other international dishes. The restaurant has a stunning location overlooking the sea and is popular among couples and groups.

Blueberries Café Bar: This café is located near the harbor in Paphos and offers a range of breakfast, lunch, and dinner options, as well as coffee and desserts. The café has a relaxed and cozy atmosphere and is popular among couples and groups.

Paphos Nightlife

Paphos is a popular tourist destination located on the southwestern coast of Cyprus. It is known for its beautiful beaches, historical landmarks, and vibrant nightlife. Paphos has a lively nightlife scene that caters to different tastes and preferences. Whether you are looking for a quiet evening out or a wild night of partying, there is something for everyone in Paphos.

One of the main areas for nightlife in Paphos is the Kato Paphos district, which is located near the harbor. Here you will find a variety of bars, clubs, and restaurants that are open until the early hours of the morning. The area has a laid-back atmosphere and is perfect for a relaxing evening out with friends.

For those looking for a more upbeat atmosphere, there are several nightclubs in Paphos that offer a great party experience. The most popular nightclubs in Paphos include Castle Club, Club Deep, and Carwash Club. These clubs feature live music, DJ performances, and dancing until the early hours of the morning. They are also known for their themed parties and events, such as beach parties and foam parties.

If you prefer a more low-key nightlife experience, there are several bars and pubs in Paphos where you can enjoy a drink and good conversation. Some of the popular bars in Paphos include The Old Fishing Shack, The Lodge, and The Britannia. These bars offer a relaxed and comfortable atmosphere, where you can enjoy a drink with friends and meet new people.

For those who enjoy live music, Paphos has several venues that feature local and international performers. The most popular live music venues in Paphos include The Paphos Amphitheatre and The Paphos Aphrodite Festival. These venues host a variety of events throughout the year, including concerts, music festivals, and theater performances.

Paphos also has a variety of restaurants and cafes that are open late into the night. Whether you are looking for traditional Cypriot cuisine or international flavors, you will find plenty of options in Paphos. Some of the popular restaurants in Paphos include The Rib Shack, The Farmyard Restaurant, and The Lodge Restaurant.

In addition to the nightlife options in Kato Paphos, there are also several other areas in Paphos that offer a great nightlife experience. The Coral Bay area, located about 15 minutes away from Paphos, is home to several bars and restaurants that offer a more upscale atmosphere. The Tomb of the Kings area is also known for its nightlife scene, with several bars and clubs that cater to a younger crowd.

One of the best things about Paphos nightlife is that it is not limited to just one area. Visitors can explore different parts of the city and discover new bars, clubs, and restaurants to enjoy. Additionally, Paphos is known for its friendly and welcoming atmosphere, which makes it easy to meet new people and make new friends.

Another popular aspect of Paphos nightlife is the beach parties. During the summer months, many of the bars and clubs in Paphos host beach parties where visitors can dance the night away under the stars. These parties are a great way to experience the local culture and meet other travelers.

For those who want to experience the traditional music and dance of Cyprus, there are several places in Paphos that offer live performances. One such place is the Ouzeri tou Thanasi, located in the Old Town of Paphos. Here visitors can enjoy traditional Cypriot music and dance while sipping on ouzo and tasting delicious meze.

In addition to the nightlife scene in Paphos, there are also several cultural and historical landmarks that are open late into the evening. The Paphos Archaeological Park, for example, is open until 7:30 pm during the summer months, allowing visitors to explore the ancient ruins of the city at night.

Paphos nightlife is diverse, exciting, and welcoming. Whether you are looking for a relaxed evening out or a wild night of partying, Paphos has something to offer. With its beautiful beaches, historical landmarks, and lively atmosphere, Paphos is the perfect destination for anyone looking to experience the best of Cyprus nightlife.

Day trip from Paphos

Paphos is a beautiful coastal town located on the southwestern coast of Cyprus. It is known for its historical landmarks, beautiful beaches, and lively nightlife. While there is plenty to see and do in Paphos, there are also several day trips that visitors can take to explore other parts of the island. Here are some of the best day trips from Paphos:

Akamas Peninsula - The Akamas Peninsula is a protected national park located about an hour's drive from Paphos. It is home to some of the most beautiful beaches and natural landscapes in Cyprus, including the famous Blue Lagoon. Visitors can explore the park on foot or by jeep safari and enjoy the stunning views and crystal-clear waters.

Troodos Mountains - The Troodos Mountains are located in the center of Cyprus and are a popular day trip destination from Paphos. The mountains are home to several picturesque villages, including Omodos and Platres, and offer visitors a chance to escape the heat and enjoy cooler temperatures. The area is also known for its beautiful hiking trails and stunning views.

Limassol - Limassol is the second-largest city in Cyprus and is located about an hour's drive from Paphos. It is known for its beautiful beaches, historic landmarks, and lively atmosphere. Visitors can explore the Old Town, visit the Limassol Castle, or enjoy a day at the beach.

Nicosia - Nicosia is the capital city of Cyprus and is located about two hours' drive from Paphos. It is a fascinating city that offers a blend of modern and traditional architecture, culture, and history. Visitors can explore the Old City, visit the Cyprus Museum, or enjoy a traditional Cypriot meal at one of the many restaurants.

Larnaca - Larnaca is a coastal city located on the southeastern coast of Cyprus and is about a two-hour drive from Paphos. It is known for its beautiful beaches, vibrant nightlife, and historical landmarks, including the Hala Sultan Tekke Mosque and the St. Lazarus Church.

Petra tou Romiou - Petra tou Romiou, also known as Aphrodite's Rock, is a famous landmark located about 30 minutes' drive from Paphos. According to mythology, this is the place where the Greek goddess Aphrodite was born from the sea foam. The rock formation is a popular spot for swimming and snorkeling, and visitors can also enjoy the beautiful views of the coastline.

Pissouri Bay - Pissouri Bay is a beautiful beach located about 30 minutes' drive from Paphos. The beach is surrounded by stunning cliffs and offers clear waters that are perfect for swimming and snorkeling. Visitors can also enjoy a range of water sports, including windsurfing and jet skiing.

Tombs of the Kings - The Tombs of the Kings is an archaeological site located in Paphos that dates back to the 4th century BC. The site contains a complex of underground tombs that were used by wealthy families during the Hellenistic and Roman periods. Visitors can explore the tombs and learn about the history of the site.

Curium - Curium is an ancient city located on the southwestern coast of Cyprus, about an hour's drive from Paphos. The site contains the remains of a Greco-Roman theater, a stadium, and a bathhouse, among other structures. Visitors can explore the site and learn about the history of this ancient city.

Kykkos Monastery - Kykkos Monastery is located in the Troodos Mountains and is one of the most important religious sites in Cyprus. The monastery dates back to the 11th century and is home to a range of religious artifacts and treasures. Visitors can explore the monastery and learn about the history and culture of Cyprus.

Where to Relax and Enjoy

Paphos is a great place to relax and enjoy the beautiful Mediterranean climate. Whether you are looking for a day at the beach or a spa day, there are plenty of options available at different price points.

Beaches: Paphos is home to several beautiful beaches, some of which are free to access, while others charge a small fee. The most popular beaches in the area include Coral Bay, which has golden sand and clear waters, and Lara Beach, which is a protected turtle nesting site. Visitors can also check out the quieter beaches of Latchi, which has crystal-clear waters, and the pebble beach of Aphrodite's Rock.

Spas: There are several spas in Paphos where visitors can relax and enjoy a range of treatments. The prices for spa services vary depending on the type of treatment and the spa's location. The most luxurious spas in Paphos are usually located in five-star hotels, such as the Elysium Spa, which offers a range of treatments starting from €65 for a 30-minute massage, and the

Anassa Spa, which offers a range of treatments starting from €120.

For those looking for a more affordable option, there are several day spas in Paphos that offer treatments at more affordable prices. The Aphrodite Hills Spa, for example, offers a range of treatments starting from €30 for a 30-minute massage.

Restaurants: Paphos is home to a range of restaurants that offer a variety of cuisines at different price points. Visitors can enjoy traditional Cypriot dishes at local tavernas, or they can try international cuisine at more upscale restaurants.

For those on a budget, there are several local tavernas that offer traditional Cypriot dishes at affordable prices. One popular option is To Steki Tou Thanasi, which is known for its grilled meats and meze dishes at reasonable prices.

For those looking for a more upscale dining experience, there are several fine-dining restaurants in Paphos, such as the Yialos Taverna, which offers fresh seafood and Mediterranean cuisine at prices starting from €30 per person.

Bars: Paphos is also known for its vibrant nightlife, and there are several bars and nightclubs in the town where visitors can enjoy drinks and music. The prices for drinks and entry fees vary depending on the establishment and the time of year.

For those on a budget, there are several local bars in Paphos that offer affordable drinks and a relaxed atmosphere. One popular option is the Wooden Crest Bar, which offers cheap drinks and live music.

For those looking for a more upscale experience, there are several high-end bars in Paphos, such as the Sunset

Lounge, which offers stunning views of the sunset and a range of cocktails starting from €10.

Outdoor activities: Apart from beaches and spas, Paphos offers a range of outdoor activities for visitors to enjoy. These include hiking, cycling, and water sports. Prices for these activities vary depending on the provider and the season. For those looking for a fun day out, Paphos Waterpark is a great option. The park offers a range of water slides and pools, as well as restaurants and a souvenir shop. Tickets start from €29 for adults and €16 for children.

Another popular outdoor activity is quad biking. Visitors can explore the countryside and enjoy the stunning views of the coastline on a quad bike. Prices for quad biking tours start from €40 per person for a two-hour tour.

For those looking for a more active adventure, there are several hiking and cycling trails in the area. The Akamas Peninsula is a popular spot for hiking and offers stunning views of the coastline. Cycling tours are also available, and prices start from €30 per person for a half-day tour.

Accommodation: Paphos offers a range of accommodation options to suit different budgets. Visitors can choose from five-star hotels, self-catering apartments, and budget-friendly hostels. For those looking for a luxurious stay, the five-star hotels in Paphos offer a range of amenities, including spa services, fine-dining restaurants, and private beaches. Prices for five-star hotels start from €150 per night.

For those looking for a more affordable option, self-catering apartments and hostels are available at lower prices. One popular option is the Smartline Paphos Hotel, which offers affordable rooms and a range of amenities, including a swimming pool, restaurant, and bar.

Larnaca

Larnaca is a city located on the southern coast of Cyprus, a small island country in the eastern Mediterranean. It is the third-largest city in Cyprus after Nicosia and Limassol and is a popular destination for tourists from all over the world. The history of Larnaca dates back to ancient times, with evidence of settlements dating as far back as the 13th century BC. Over the centuries, the city has been ruled by various empires and civilizations, including the Persians, Egyptians, and Romans. In the Middle Ages, Larnaca was part of the Byzantine Empire and later the Venetian Republic.

Today, Larnaca is a vibrant city with a mix of old and new architecture, beautiful beaches, and a bustling nightlife. Visitors can explore the old town with its narrow streets and traditional houses or visit the Larnaca Salt Lake, a large lake that is home to a variety of bird species. One of the most popular attractions in Larnaca is the Hala Sultan Tekke, a mosque built in honor of the prophet Mohammed's aunt. It is a significant religious site for Muslims and is visited by thousands of pilgrims every year.

Larnaca is also known for its beautiful beaches, including Finikoudes Beach, which is located in the heart of the city and is famous for its palm tree-lined promenade. Other popular beaches in Larnaca include Mackenzie Beach and Dhekelia Beach.

Top Attractions

Larnaca is a city full of history, culture, and natural beauty, with plenty of attractions to keep visitors entertained. Here are some of the top attractions in

Larnaca and how visitors can access them:

Finikoudes Beach: This is the most popular beach in Larnaca and is located in the heart of the city. Visitors can easily access the beach by foot, as it is just a few minutes' walk from the city center. There are also several bus stops nearby, making it easy to reach by public transportation.

Hala Sultan Tekke: This is a significant religious site for Muslims and is located about 6 km west of Larnaca. Visitors can access the mosque by car or taxi, and there is also a bus stop nearby.

Larnaca Salt Lake: This is a large lake located just outside the city center and is a popular spot for bird watching. Visitors can access the lake by car, bike, or bus.

St. Lazarus Church: This is a beautiful church located in the heart of Larnaca's old town. Visitors can access the church by foot, as it is just a short walk from the city center. There are also several bus stops nearby.

Larnaca Fort: This is an impressive fort located at the southern end of Finikoudes Beach. Visitors can access the fort by foot, as it is just a short walk from the city center. There are also several bus stops nearby.

Kamares Aqueduct: This is an ancient aqueduct located about 6 km northwest of Larnaca. Visitors can access the aqueduct by car or taxi, and there is also a bus stop nearby.

Mackenzie Beach: This is a popular beach located about 2 km southeast of Larnaca. Visitors can access the beach by car, bike, or bus.

Larnaca Archaeological Museum: This museum is located in the center of Larnaca and houses a collection of ancient artifacts, including pottery, jewelry, and sculptures. Visitors can access the museum by foot or by bus.

Pierides Museum: This is another museum located in the center of Larnaca and features a collection of Cypriot antiquities and art from the Byzantine period. Visitors can access the museum by foot or by bus.

Stavrovouni Monastery: This is a Greek Orthodox monastery located about 20 km southwest of Larnaca, on top of a mountain. Visitors can access the monastery by car or taxi, and there are also several tour companies that offer guided visits.

Lefkara Village: This is a traditional Cypriot village located about 20 km northwest of Larnaca, known for its lace and silverware. Visitors can access the village by car or taxi, and there are also several tour companies that offer guided visits.

Camel Park: This is a popular family-friendly attraction located about 20 km west of Larnaca, where visitors can ride camels and enjoy other activities, such as archery and mini-golf. Visitors can access the park by car or taxi.

In addition to these attractions, visitors to Larnaca can also enjoy a variety of water sports, such as windsurfing and kiteboarding, at several locations along the coast. The city also has a vibrant food and drink scene, with plenty of restaurants and bars serving traditional Cypriot cuisine and international dishes.

Where to Eat

Larnaca is a city that offers a variety of dining options, from traditional Cypriot cuisine to international dishes. Here are some suggestions for where to eat in Larnaca:

Zephyros Restaurant: This restaurant is located on Finikoudes Beach and offers stunning views of the sea. The menu features traditional Cypriot dishes, such as grilled fish and souvlaki, as well as international options. The restaurant also has a bar area, where visitors can enjoy cocktails and live music.

To Kafe Tis Chrysanthi's: This is a family-run restaurant located in the heart of Larnaca's old town, known for its traditional Cypriot meze. The restaurant also offers vegetarian and vegan options, and visitors can enjoy their meal in a cozy courtyard setting.

Militzis: This is another traditional Cypriot restaurant located in the city center, known for its grilled meat dishes and meze. The restaurant also has a lovely outdoor seating area, perfect for enjoying the warm Mediterranean weather.

The Brewery: This is a popular bar and restaurant located near the Larnaca Marina, known for its craft beers and pub food. The menu features burgers, sandwiches, and salads, as well as vegetarian options.

Mousiki Taverna: This is a charming restaurant located in the village of Lefkara, known for its traditional Cypriot dishes and live music. Visitors can enjoy their meal in a cozy indoor or outdoor setting, surrounded by the village's picturesque architecture.

To Koutourou: This is a seafood restaurant located on Mackenzie Beach, known for its fresh fish and seafood dishes. Visitors can enjoy their meal on a terrace overlooking the sea, making it the perfect spot for a romantic dinner.

Piatsa Gourounaki: This is a popular restaurant located in the city center, known for its grilled pork dishes. The menu also features traditional Cypriot meze, salads, and vegetarian options. The restaurant has a cozy indoor and outdoor seating area, perfect for a casual meal with friends or family.

To Perasma: This is a charming restaurant located in the village of Kiti, known for its traditional Cypriot dishes and homemade desserts. The restaurant has a lovely outdoor seating area, surrounded by lush greenery and a peaceful atmosphere.

Alasia Restaurant: This is a fine dining restaurant located in a boutique hotel in the city center, known for its creative Mediterranean cuisine. The menu features seasonal and locally-sourced ingredients, and the restaurant also has an extensive wine list.

Mer Bleue Beach Restaurant: This is a beachfront restaurant located on the outskirts of Larnaca, known for its fresh seafood and stunning views of the Mediterranean. Visitors can enjoy their meal on a terrace overlooking the sea, making it the perfect spot for a special occasion.

To Kypriako: This is a family-run tavern located in the village of Pervolia, known for its traditional Cypriot dishes and warm hospitality. The menu features meze, grilled meat dishes, and homemade desserts, and visitors can enjoy their meal in a cozy indoor or outdoor setting.

Larnaca Nightlife

Visitors to Larnaca can enjoy a vibrant nightlife scene with plenty of bars, clubs, and restaurants to choose from. Here are some places where visitors can experience Larnaca's nightlife:

Finikoudes Beach - This beach is a popular destination for both locals and tourists, and it comes alive at night with its many bars and restaurants. Prices for drinks and food are generally reasonable.

Mckenzie Beach - This area is also popular for its bars and nightclubs. Prices for drinks and food can be slightly higher than at other places in Larnaca, but still relatively affordable.

Zephyros - This trendy bar and restaurant is located in the heart of Larnaca's Old Town and is popular for its cocktails and live music. Prices for drinks and food are moderate, with cocktails priced around €8-€10.

Savino Rock Bar - This popular bar features live music and DJ sets and is located in Larnaca's shopping district. Prices for drinks are reasonable, with beers starting at around €3.

The Brewery - This bar offers a wide selection of beers and is known for its friendly atmosphere. Prices for drinks are reasonable, with beers starting at around €3.

Galu Seaside - This beachfront restaurant and bar is known for its beautiful views and delicious food. Prices for drinks and food can be slightly higher than at other places in Larnaca, with cocktails priced around €10-€12.

Alea Cafe Lounge Bar - This modern lounge bar is located in the center of Larnaca and offers a relaxed atmosphere, making it a great place to unwind after a long day of exploring.

Prices for drinks and food are moderate, with cocktails priced around €8-€10.

Deja Vu Bar - This lively bar is popular among both locals and tourists, offering a great selection of drinks and live music. Prices for drinks are reasonable, with beers starting at around €3.

Maqam Al Sultan - This Middle Eastern restaurant and shisha bar is a unique experience for those looking for something different. Prices for food and shisha are reasonable, with shisha starting at around €10.

Alion Beach Hotel - This luxury hotel offers a beachfront bar and restaurant with stunning views of the Mediterranean Sea. Prices for drinks and food can be slightly higher than at other places in Larnaca, with cocktails priced around €12-€15.

Castle Club - This popular nightclub is located in the heart of Larnaca's nightlife district and offers multiple rooms with different music genres, making it a great place for dancing and partying. Prices for drinks are reasonable, with beers starting at around €3.

Havana Bar - This Cuban-inspired bar is a great place to enjoy a cocktail and some live music. Prices for drinks are moderate, with cocktails priced around €8-€10.

Where to Eat

Visitors to Larnaca can enjoy a wide variety of dining options, from traditional Cypriot tavernas to modern restaurants with international cuisine. Here are some places where visitors can eat in Larnaca:

To Kazani - This traditional Cypriot taverna is located in the heart of Larnaca's old town and offers a wide range of local dishes, such as kleftiko, moussaka, and souvlaki. Prices are reasonable, with main dishes priced around €12-€15.

Militzis - This popular seafood restaurant is located on the Finikoudes promenade and offers a great selection of fresh fish and seafood dishes. Prices can be slightly higher than at other places in Larnaca, with main dishes priced around €20-€25.

Piatsa Gourounaki - This rustic taverna is located in Larnaca's shopping district and offers a great selection of grilled meats and meze dishes. Prices are reasonable, with main dishes priced around €12-€15.

Art Cafe 1900 - This trendy cafe and restaurant is located in Larnaca's old town and offers a fusion of Mediterranean and international cuisine. Prices are moderate, with main dishes priced around €15-€20.

Kalamies Beach Restaurant - This beachfront restaurant is located in Protaras, a short drive from Larnaca, and offers a great selection of seafood and Mediterranean dishes. Prices can be slightly higher than at other places in Larnaca, with main dishes priced around €20-€25.

Zygi Fish Tavern - This traditional seafood taverna is located in the small fishing village of Zygi, a short drive from Larnaca, and offers a great selection of fresh fish and seafood dishes. Prices are reasonable, with main dishes priced around €20-€25.

Ttappis Tavern - This traditional Cypriot taverna is located in Larnaca's old town and offers a great selection of local dishes, such as moussaka, kleftiko, and afelia. Prices are reasonable, with main dishes priced around €12-€15.

To Ploumin - This traditional Cypriot taverna is located in the village of Skarinou, a short drive from Larnaca, and offers a great selection of meze dishes. Prices are reasonable, with meze priced around €20 per person.

The Corner Restaurant - This modern restaurant is located in Larnaca's shopping district and offers a fusion of Mediterranean and international cuisine. Prices are moderate, with main dishes priced around €15-€20.

Pyxida Fish Tavern - This traditional seafood taverna is located in Larnaca's old port and offers a great selection of fresh fish and seafood dishes. Prices are reasonable, with main dishes priced around €20-€25.

Overall, Larnaca offers a diverse range of dining options to suit all tastes and budgets. Visitors can expect to find reasonably priced traditional Cypriot tavernas, as well as more modern restaurants with Mediterranean and international cuisine.

Day trip from Larnaca

Larnaca is a great base for exploring the island of Cyprus, as there are many interesting day trip options within easy reach. Here are some ideas for day trips from Larnaca:

Nicosia - Cyprus' capital city is just a short drive from Larnaca and offers a fascinating mix of Greek and Turkish culture. Visitors can explore the walled Old Town, visit the Cyprus Museum, and see the famous Green Line that divides the city into Greek and Turkish sectors.

Limassol - This coastal city is known for its lively atmosphere and long sandy beaches. Visitors can explore the old town, visit the medieval castle, and take a stroll along the promenade.

Ayia Napa - This popular tourist destination is located on the east coast of Cyprus and is known for its beautiful beaches and vibrant nightlife. Visitors can enjoy water sports, visit the Ayia Napa Monastery, and explore the Cape Greco National Forest Park.

Troodos Mountains - The Troodos Mountains are a scenic region in the center of Cyprus, offering beautiful landscapes, quaint villages, and historic monasteries. Visitors can go hiking, explore the Kykkos Monastery, and see the famous painted churches of the region.

Paphos - This coastal city on the west coast of Cyprus is known for its ancient archaeological sites and picturesque harbor. Visitors can explore the Paphos Archaeological Park, visit the Tombs of the Kings, and see the famous Aphrodite's Rock.

Lefkara - This picturesque village is located in the foothills of the Troodos Mountains and is known for its traditional lace-making and silverwork. Visitors can explore the narrow streets, visit the local museums, and try the local Cypriot cuisine.

Famagusta - This historic city is located in the northern part of Cyprus and is known for its well-preserved medieval walls and buildings. Visitors can explore the Othello Castle, visit the Lala Mustafa Pasha Mosque, and see the famous ghost town of Varosha.

Cape Greco - Located on the southeastern tip of Cyprus, Cape Greco is a protected national park with stunning cliffs, sea caves, and crystal-clear waters. Visitors can enjoy hiking, swimming, and snorkeling, and see the famous Sea Caves and Love Bridge.

Kourion - This ancient city is located on the south coast of Cyprus and features well-preserved Greco-Roman ruins, including a theater, baths, and mosaics. Visitors can also enjoy beautiful views of the Mediterranean Sea.

Larnaca Salt Lake - This large salt lake is located just outside of Larnaca and is home to a variety of bird species, including flamingos. Visitors can enjoy a peaceful walk or bike ride around the lake and observe the wildlife.

Kiti Village - This charming village is located just a short drive from Larnaca and is known for its beautiful church, Panagia Angeloktisti, which features stunning Byzantine mosaics.

Choirokoitia - This UNESCO World Heritage Site is located in the Larnaca District and features well-preserved ruins of a Neolithic settlement dating back to 7000 BC. Visitors can explore the archaeological site and learn about the ancient culture of Cyprus.

Where Relax and Enjoy

There are many places in Larnaca and the surrounding areas where visitors can relax and enjoy themselves. Here are some highlights:

Beaches - Larnaca has many beautiful beaches, including Finikoudes Beach, McKenzie Beach, and Yanathes Beach. Visitors can relax on the sand, swim in the crystal-clear waters, and enjoy the sun. Prices for beach loungers and umbrellas vary, but can typically be rented for a few euros per day.

Zenon Spa - Located in the heart of Larnaca, Zenon Spa offers a range of relaxing spa treatments, including massages, facials, and body wraps. Prices vary depending on the treatment, but start at around €50 for a massage.

Hala Sultan Tekke - This historic mosque is located on the shore of Larnaca Salt Lake and is a peaceful place to relax and reflect. Visitors can enjoy the beautiful architecture and serene surroundings for free.

Lefkara Village - This charming village is located in the Troodos Mountains and is known for its traditional lace-making and silverwork. Visitors can stroll through the narrow streets, enjoy a meal at a local taverna, and shop for souvenirs. Prices for meals vary, but can typically range from €10-€20 per person.

Stavrovouni Monastery - This historic monastery is located on a hilltop just outside of Larnaca and offers beautiful views of the surrounding countryside. Visitors can explore the monastery and enjoy the peaceful surroundings for free.

CTO Beach - This secluded beach is located just outside of Larnaca and is a popular spot for locals and tourists alike. Visitors can relax on the sand, swim in the calm waters, and enjoy the stunning views. Prices for beach loungers and umbrellas vary, but can typically be rented for a few euros per day.

Park of Faneromeni - This park is located in the center of Larnaca and offers a peaceful oasis in the middle of the city. Visitors can relax on the grass, enjoy a picnic, and admire the historic monuments. Admission to the park is free.

Mackenzie Beach - Mackenzie Beach is a popular spot for locals and tourists alike, and offers a lively atmosphere with many bars and restaurants. Visitors can relax on the beach during the day and enjoy the nightlife in the evening. Prices for beach loungers and umbrellas vary, but can typically be rented for a few euros per day.

Larnaca Marina - The Larnaca Marina offers a beautiful setting for a relaxing evening stroll. Visitors can enjoy the views of the boats and the sea, and dine at one of the many restaurants and cafes along the waterfront. Prices for meals vary, but can typically range from €10-€20 per person.

Ayia Napa - Ayia Napa is located about 45 minutes from Larnaca and is known for its beautiful beaches and lively nightlife. Visitors can relax on the sandy beaches during the day and enjoy the many bars and clubs in the evening. Prices for beach loungers and umbrellas vary, but can typically be rented for a few euros per day.

Troodos Mountains - The Troodos Mountains are located about 2 hours from Larnaca and offer a beautiful setting for a relaxing day trip. Visitors can enjoy the scenic drive, go hiking, and visit the traditional villages in the area. Prices for meals and activities vary, but many are affordable and accessible to all visitors.

Kamares Aqueduct - The Kamares Aqueduct is a historic landmark located just outside of Larnaca, and offers a beautiful setting for a peaceful walk. Visitors can admire the beautiful architecture and enjoy the peaceful surroundings for free.

Ayia Napa

Ayia Napa is a town located on the southeastern coast of the Mediterranean island of Cyprus. The town is known for its stunning beaches, vibrant nightlife, and annual festivals. In this response, we will discuss the history, economy, and festivals of Ayia Napa.

History: Ayia Napa's history dates back to ancient times when the town was known as "Agia Napa," which translates to "holy wooded valley." The town was believed to be the site of a temple dedicated to the goddess Artemis. During the Byzantine era, the town became a monastic settlement, and the monastery of Ayia Napa was built. The monastery played a significant role in the town's development, as it attracted pilgrims and visitors from all over the island. In the 20th century, Ayia Napa was a small fishing village until tourism began to boom in the 1980s.

Economy: Today, tourism is the main driver of Ayia Napa's economy. The town attracts millions of tourists every year, who come to enjoy its beautiful beaches, crystal-clear waters, and lively nightlife. The town has also invested in other tourism-related activities such as water sports, diving, and cultural events. Ayia Napa is also home to a number of hotels, restaurants, and bars, which provide employment opportunities for local residents.

Festival: Ayia Napa hosts an annual festival called the Ayia Napa International Festival. The festival takes place in September and features a range of cultural activities, including music, dance, and theater performances. The festival also showcases traditional Cypriot cuisine and handicrafts. Visitors can also enjoy a range of activities, including sports tournaments, exhibitions, and workshops. The festival is an excellent opportunity for visitors to experience the island's rich culture and traditions.

Ayia Napa is a beautiful town with a rich history, a booming tourism industry, and an exciting annual festival. Its stunning beaches, crystal-clear waters, and lively nightlife make it a popular destination for tourists from around the world.

Top Attractions

Here are some of the top attractions in Ayia Napa:

Nissi Beach: Nissi Beach is one of the most famous beaches in Ayia Napa, known for its crystal-clear turquoise waters, white sand, and lively atmosphere. It's an excellent spot for swimming, sunbathing, and water sports.

Cape Greco National Forest Park: Cape Greco National Forest Park is a protected natural area located on the southeastern tip of Cyprus. It's a popular spot for hiking, cycling, and picnicking, and offers stunning views of the Mediterranean Sea.

Ayia Napa Monastery: The Ayia Napa Monastery is a 16th-century monastery located in the heart of the town. It's a beautiful example of Venetian architecture and is still in use as a church today.

Thalassa Municipal Museum: The Thalassa Municipal Museum is dedicated to the history and culture of the sea. It features exhibits on marine life, fishing traditions, and the island's maritime history.

Water World Waterpark: Water World Waterpark is a popular attraction for families and thrill-seekers. It features a range of water slides, pools, and attractions, including a wave pool and lazy river.

Ayia Napa Sculpture Park: Ayia Napa Sculpture Park is an open-air museum featuring a collection of contemporary sculptures by Cypriot and international artists. It's a beautiful spot to take a stroll and admire the art.

Ayia Napa Harbour: Ayia Napa Harbour is a picturesque spot to watch the fishing boats come and go, or to take a boat tour of the coast. There are also a number of restaurants and bars with outdoor seating where you can enjoy a meal or drink while taking in the view.

Ayia Napa Aqueduct: The Ayia Napa Aqueduct is a historical landmark and a great place to take a scenic walk. The aqueduct was built in the 18th century to supply water to the town and is made up of a series of arches.

Makronissos Tombs: The Makronissos Tombs are a series of underground tombs dating back to the Hellenistic period. The tombs are carved into the rock and feature elaborate decorations and inscriptions.

Love Bridge: The Love Bridge is a natural rock formation located near Nissi Beach. Legend has it that couples who cross the bridge together will have a long and happy relationship.

Ayia Napa Sea Caves: The Ayia Napa Sea Caves are a network of underwater caves and tunnels located along the coast. They're a popular spot for diving and snorkeling and offer a unique glimpse into the island's marine life.

Ayia Napa Square: Ayia Napa Square is the heart of the town's nightlife scene. It's a lively area with bars, restaurants, and clubs, and is a popular spot for partygoers.

Overall, Ayia Napa has something for everyone, whether you're looking for natural beauty, historical landmarks, or a fun night out. Its mix of attractions makes it a great destination for families, couples, and solo travelers alike.

Where to Eat

Ayia Napa has a range of dining options to suit every taste and budget. Here are some places visitors can eat, including their prices:

Sage Restaurant: Sage Restaurant is a Mediterranean restaurant located in the center of Ayia Napa. The menu includes a range of traditional and modern dishes, including seafood, pasta, and meat. Prices start at around €20 for a main course.

Los Bandidos Mexican Restaurant: Los Bandidos Mexican Restaurant is a popular spot for Mexican food in Ayia Napa. The menu includes classics such as tacos, burritos, and fajitas, as well as a range of margaritas and cocktails. Prices start at around €15 for a main course.

Karousos Beach Restaurant: Karousos Beach Restaurant is a beachfront restaurant that serves Mediterranean cuisine. The menu includes fresh seafood, grilled meats, and salads. Prices start at around €18 for a main course.

Quadro: Quadro is a fine-dining restaurant located in the Napa Plaza

Hotel. The menu features creative Mediterranean cuisine, with an emphasis on fresh local ingredients. Prices start at around €30 for a main course.

Zorbas Bakery and Cafe: Zorbas Bakery and Cafe is a family-run bakery and cafe that serves traditional Cypriot pastries and coffee. Prices start at around €3 for a pastry and €2 for a coffee.

Kahlua Cafe-Bar: Kahlua Cafe-Bar is a popular spot for drinks and light bites in Ayia Napa. The menu includes a range of cocktails, beers, and sandwiches. Prices start at around €5 for a drink and €7 for a sandwich.

Hobo Mediterraneo: Hobo Mediterraneo is a beachfront restaurant that serves Mediterranean and Italian cuisine. The menu includes pasta, pizza, seafood, and meat dishes. Prices start at around €15 for a main course.

The Deck Cafe Bar: The Deck Cafe Bar is a popular spot for drinks and light bites, located in the center of Ayia Napa. The menu includes a range of cocktails, beers, and snacks. Prices start at around €5 for a drink and €8 for a snack.

Blueberries Cafe and Restaurant: Blueberries Cafe and Restaurant is a family-friendly restaurant that serves international cuisine. The menu includes burgers, salads, pasta, and pizza. Prices start at around €10 for a main course.

To Kanoni: To Kanoni is a traditional Greek tavern located in the center of Ayia Napa. The menu includes a range of Greek dishes, including moussaka, souvlaki, and stuffed peppers. Prices start at around €15 for a main course.

Wagamama: Wagamama is a chain restaurant that serves Asian-inspired cuisine. The menu includes ramen, stir-fry, and curry dishes, as well as sushi and bao buns. Prices start at around €10 for a main course.

Konnos Bay Beach Bar and Restaurant: Konnos Bay Beach Bar and Restaurant is a beachfront restaurant that serves Mediterranean cuisine. The menu includes fresh seafood, grilled meats, and salads. Prices start at around €20 for a main course.

Whether you're in the mood for fine dining or a casual meal, Ayia Napa has plenty of options to choose from. Visitors can enjoy everything from traditional Cypriot cuisine to international flavors, all at a range of prices to suit any budget.

Ayia Napa Nightlife

One of the main attractions of Ayia Napa is its vibrant and diverse nightlife, which offers a wide range of entertainment options that cater to different tastes and preferences. Whether you are looking for an all-night party, a laid-back bar, or a sophisticated club, Ayia Napa has something to offer for everyone.

The town's main nightlife hub is located in the center of the town, around the famous Ayia Napa Square. This area is packed with bars, clubs, and restaurants, which come alive after dark and stay open until the early hours of the morning. The atmosphere here is electric, with music blasting from every corner, crowds of people dancing and socializing, and a sense of excitement and freedom that is hard to find elsewhere.

For those who are looking for a more relaxed and intimate atmosphere, Ayia Napa has plenty of options too. The town has many cozy bars and taverns, where you can enjoy a quiet drink, chat with the locals, and soak in the traditional Cypriot culture.

To make the most of your Ayia Napa nightlife experience, it is important to plan ahead and choose the places that suit your taste and budget. You can start by doing some research online, reading reviews, and asking for recommendations from the locals. Many bars and clubs offer special deals and promotions, such as free entrance, discounted drinks, and VIP packages, so it's worth checking them out before you hit the town.

When it comes to getting around Ayia Napa at night, there are several options available. Walking is a great way to explore the town, as many bars and clubs are located in close proximity to each other. Taxis and buses are also available, but be aware that they can get busy and expensive during peak times.

But, the nightlife scene in Ayia Napa is not just limited to the town center. There are many other hotspots scattered around the town that are worth exploring. The popular Nissi Beach is home to several beach bars and clubs that offer a unique party experience under the stars, with the sound of the waves as the background music. Another area that is gaining popularity is the Ayia Thekla area, which boasts several trendy beach clubs and bars, where you can enjoy a sophisticated and chic nightlife experience.

When it comes to dress code, Ayia Napa is generally quite relaxed and casual, with most bars and clubs allowing you to wear casual clothing. However, some clubs do have a dress code, so it's worth checking before you go.

In terms of safety, Ayia Napa is generally a safe place to party, but it's always important to take precautions and look after yourself and your belongings. Be aware of your surroundings, avoid getting too drunk, and never leave your drinks unattended.

Day trip from Ayia Napa

If you are looking for a break from the vibrant nightlife scene in Ayia Napa, there are plenty of options for day trips that allow you to explore the beautiful surroundings and experience the rich culture and history of Cyprus. Here are some of the best day trips from Ayia Napa:

Cape Greco: Located just a few kilometers from Ayia Napa, Cape Greco is a natural park that boasts stunning sea views, dramatic cliffs, and crystal-clear waters. The area is popular for swimming, snorkeling, and diving, and there are several hiking trails that allow you to explore the park's rugged terrain and discover hidden caves and rock formations.

Famagusta: A short drive from Ayia Napa, Famagusta is a historic city that is known for its beautiful architecture and rich cultural heritage. The city's Old Town is home to several historic landmarks, including the 14th-century Venetian Walls, the Gothic-style St. Nicholas Cathedral, and the ancient Othello Castle.

Nicosia: The capital of Cyprus, Nicosia is a vibrant city that blends modernity with tradition. The city's Old Town is a maze of narrow streets and alleyways, lined with charming cafes, restaurants, and shops selling local handicrafts. Highlights include the imposing Venetian Walls, the stunning Selimiye Mosque, and the colorful Ledra Street Market.

Troodos Mountains: If you're looking for a scenic escape from the heat and crowds of Ayia Napa, the Troodos Mountains are the perfect destination. Located in the heart of Cyprus, this beautiful mountain range is home to several picturesque villages, ancient monasteries, and scenic hiking trails. The highlight is Mount Olympus, the highest peak in Cyprus, which offers stunning views of the surrounding landscape.

Larnaca: Just a short drive from Ayia Napa, Larnaca is a beautiful coastal city that is known for its palm-lined promenade, sandy beaches, and ancient ruins. Highlights include the beautiful St. Lazarus Church, the historic Kition Archaeological Site, and the bustling Finikoudes Beach, which is lined with bars, cafes, and restaurants.

When planning your day trip from Ayia Napa, it's important to consider transportation options. You can rent a car, take a bus, or book a tour with a local operator, depending on your budget and preferences. Whichever option you choose, be sure to bring plenty of water, sunscreen, and comfortable shoes, as many of these destinations involve hiking and outdoor activities.

Akamas Peninsula: The Akamas Peninsula is a beautiful nature reserve located on the northwest coast of Cyprus, around a 2-hour drive from Ayia Napa. The peninsula boasts a unique landscape of rugged coastline, sandy beaches, and rolling hills, and is home to a diverse range of flora and fauna. Visitors can enjoy hiking, cycling, and swimming, and can explore the area's ancient ruins and traditional villages.

Paphos: Located on the southwest coast of Cyprus, around a 2-hour drive from Ayia Napa, Paphos is a popular destination that is known for its beautiful beaches, historic landmarks, and vibrant nightlife. Highlights include the Paphos Archaeological Park, which is home to several ancient ruins, including the Roman Amphitheater and the House of Dionysus, and the bustling Kato Paphos district, which is lined with bars, clubs, and restaurants.

Zenobia Wreck: Scuba diving enthusiasts will love the opportunity to explore the Zenobia Wreck, which is located off the coast of Larnaca, around a 40-minute drive from Ayia Napa. The Zenobia was a Swedish ferry that sank in 1980, and today lies in around 40 meters of water, offering a unique and fascinating underwater adventure.

Kykkos Monastery: Located in the Troodos Mountains, around a 2-hour drive from Ayia Napa, the Kykkos Monastery is one of the most important religious sites in Cyprus. The monastery dates back to the 11th century and is home to a stunning array of religious artifacts, including icons, relics, and murals. Visitors can also enjoy hiking in the surrounding mountains and exploring nearby villages.

Aphrodite's Rock: According to legend, Aphrodite, the goddess of love, was born from the sea foam that washed ashore on the rocks near Paphos. Today, the spot is known as Aphrodite's Rock, and is a popular destination for visitors seeking a romantic and picturesque experience. The area boasts stunning sea views, crystal-clear waters, and several hiking trails that allow you to explore the rugged coastline.

Where Relax and Enjoy

If you're looking for a relaxing day out during your visit to Ayia Napa, there are plenty of options available to suit all budgets. Here are some of the top places to unwind and enjoy yourself in and around Ayia Napa, along with their prices:

Nissi Beach: One of the most popular beaches in Ayia Napa, Nissi Beach boasts white sands, crystal-clear waters, and a lively atmosphere. Visitors can relax on sun loungers (around €2-€3 each) or try their hand at water sports, such as jet skiing and parasailing (prices vary depending on activity).

Makronissos Beach: A quieter alternative to Nissi Beach, Makronissos Beach offers a more peaceful and secluded setting. Visitors can rent sun loungers and umbrellas (around €2-€3 each) or enjoy a leisurely swim in the clear waters.

WaterWorld Waterpark: Located just outside of Ayia Napa, WaterWorld is a popular destination for families and thrill-seekers. The park features a range of water slides, pools, and attractions, as well as restaurants and snack bars. Ticket prices start at around €35 per person for a full day.

Ayia Napa Sculpture Park: A tranquil and picturesque park that showcases the work of local artists, the Ayia Napa Sculpture Park is free to visit and offers a peaceful escape from the hustle and bustle of the town.

Ayia Napa Monastery: A historic and cultural landmark, the Ayia Napa Monastery is a must-visit for anyone interested in the history of Cyprus. Visitors can explore the beautiful grounds and chapel for free.

Konnos Bay: Located a short drive from Ayia Napa, Konnos Bay is a secluded and tranquil beach that offers stunning sea views and crystal-clear waters. Visitors can rent sun loungers and umbrellas (around €2-€3 each) or simply relax on the sandy shores.

Parko Paliatso Fun Fair & Luna Park: A fun-filled destination for families, the Parko Paliatso Fun Fair & Luna Park offers a range of attractions and rides, as well as restaurants and snack bars. Ticket prices start at around €2 per ride.

Cavo Greco National Park: A beautiful and rugged natural park located just outside of Ayia Napa, Cavo Greco offers stunning sea views, hiking trails, and hidden coves. Visitors can explore the park for free and enjoy a picnic or swim in the crystal-clear waters.

Cape Greco Sea Caves: Located within the Cavo Greco National Park, the Cape Greco Sea Caves are a popular destination for snorkeling and diving enthusiasts. Visitors can explore the underwater caves and see a range of marine life. Prices for snorkeling or diving tours vary depending on the provider.

Ayia Napa Harbour: A picturesque spot in the heart of Ayia Napa, the harbor is a great place to relax and people-watch. Visitors can enjoy a meal or drink at one of the many restaurants and bars, or simply take a stroll and admire the boats.

Protaras Coastal Promenade: A scenic walking trail that stretches along the coastline from Ayia Napa to Protaras, the Protaras Coastal Promenade offers stunning sea views and a chance to explore the local area on foot. The trail is free to use and there are plenty of opportunities to stop for a drink or snack along the way.

Ayia Thekla Beach: A quieter alternative to the more popular beaches in Ayia Napa, Ayia Thekla Beach offers a peaceful setting and calm waters. Visitors can rent sun loungers and umbrellas (around €2-€3 each) or simply relax on the sandy shore.

Thalassa Museum: A fascinating museum that explores the history and culture of the sea and seafaring, the Thalassa Museum is a must-visit for anyone interested in the maritime heritage of Cyprus. Admission costs €3 per person.

Parko Akropolis: A family-friendly amusement park located in the nearby town of Paralimni, Parko Akropolis offers a range of attractions and rides, as well as restaurants and snack bars. Ticket prices start at around €2 per ride.

Kalamies Beach: Located a short drive from Ayia Napa, Kalamies Beach is a picturesque and family-friendly beach with calm waters and golden sand. Visitors can rent sun loungers and umbrellas (around €2-€3 each) or enjoy a swim in the crystal-clear waters.

Chapter 4: Shopping

Souvenirs and Local Products

One of the best ways to remember your visit to Cyprus is by bringing back some souvenirs or local products that represent the island's unique culture and traditions. When it comes to souvenirs in Cyprus, you will find a wide variety of items, including handmade lace, pottery, olive wood products, and traditional clothing such as the famous Cypriot woven fabrics, Lefkaritika. The best place to find these souvenirs is at local markets, tourist shops, and souvenir stores located in the main tourist areas.

One of the most famous markets in Cyprus is the Old Town Market in Nicosia. The market offers a range of items, from local handicrafts to traditional food products, including Cyprus Delight, also known as Turkish Delight, and Halloumi cheese. The market is located in the heart of the Old Town, and it's easily accessible by public transport or taxi.

In addition to the Old Town Market, you can find souvenir shops and tourist stores in all major tourist areas, including Limassol, Paphos, and Ayia Napa. These shops offer a range of souvenirs and local products, including hand-painted ceramics, handmade silver jewellery, and traditional Cypriot sweets.

If you are looking for local food products, the best places to visit are local markets and shops that specialize in traditional Cypriot food. You can find these shops in most towns and villages, and they offer a range of local products, including olive oil, honey, wine, and traditional sweets. Some of the most popular local products in Cyprus include:

Commandaria wine: This sweet dessert wine is made from sun-dried grapes and is one of the oldest wines in the world.

Halloumi cheese: This salty, semi-hard cheese is made from sheep and goat's milk and is a staple in Cypriot cuisine.

Loukoumia: Also known as Cyprus Delight, these sweet, chewy treats are made from starch and sugar and come in a variety of flavours.

Olive oil: Cyprus is known for its high-quality olive oil, which is produced from locally grown olives.

Apart from the souvenirs and local products mentioned above, there are many other traditional items you can find in Cyprus, such as traditional woven fabrics, leather goods, and handmade baskets. These items are usually found in local markets and shops that specialize in traditional crafts.

One popular market for traditional crafts is the Lefkara village market in the Larnaca district. The village is known for its lacework, which is made by the local women using traditional methods that have been passed down through generations. The market also offers other traditional crafts such as pottery, woodwork, and embroidery.

Another unique shopping experience in Cyprus is visiting the weekly village markets. These markets are held in various towns and villages across the island, and they offer a range of local produce, handmade crafts, and traditional products. These markets are usually held on weekends, and they provide a great opportunity to experience the local culture and mingle with the locals.

If you are looking for luxury goods, high-end fashion, and designer brands, you can visit the high-end shopping malls in the major cities such as Limassol and Nicosia. These malls offer a range of international brands and luxury goods, as well as high-quality local products and crafts.

In terms of accessing these shopping locations, most of the tourist areas have easy access to public transportation such as buses, taxis, and private shuttles. Additionally, many of the local markets and traditional craft shops are located in the town centres and are easily accessible by walking. If you are unsure about how to get to a particular shopping location, you can ask the hotel reception, tourist information centres, or the locals for directions.

Markets and Shopping Centers

Cyprus offers a variety of shopping experiences for visitors. Here are some of the markets and shopping centers in Cyprus that visitors can explore, along with some of the things they can purchase.

Ledra Street: Located in the heart of Nicosia, the capital of Cyprus, Ledra Street is a popular pedestrianized shopping area that is home to a wide range of shops, from high-end boutiques to local craft stores. Visitors can find everything from designer clothing and jewelry to handmade pottery and souvenirs. Ledra Street is easily accessible by public transportation, and visitors can also explore the nearby historic landmarks and museums.

My Mall: Located in Limassol, My Mall is one of the largest shopping centers in Cyprus, with over 100 stores spread across four levels. Visitors can find everything from fashion and beauty products to electronics and home goods. The shopping center also has a cinema, a food court, and a kids' play area. My Mall is easily accessible by car or public transportation.

Agora Market: Located in Paphos, the Agora Market is a traditional open-air market that offers a wide range of fresh produce, local meats, and handmade crafts. Visitors can purchase everything from fresh fruits and vegetables to handmade jewelry and textiles. The market is open every day except Sunday and is easily accessible by public transportation or car.

Kings Avenue Mall: Located in Paphos, the Kings Avenue Mall is a modern shopping center that offers a variety of international brands, including clothing, footwear, accessories, and electronics. The mall also has a food court, a cinema, and a kids' play area. Kings Avenue Mall is easily accessible by car or public transportation.

Larnaca Market: Located in the heart of Larnaca, the Larnaca Market is a traditional market that offers a wide range of fresh produce, seafood, and meat, as well as local crafts and souvenirs. Visitors can purchase everything from fresh fish and vegetables to handmade pottery and embroidered textiles. The market is open every day except Sunday and is easily accessible by public transportation or car.

Nicosia Municipal Market: Located in the old town of Nicosia, the Nicosia Municipal Market is a historic market that dates back to 1938. The market offers a variety of local and international products, including fresh fruits, vegetables, meats, cheeses, and spices. Visitors can also find handicrafts, souvenirs, and traditional Cypriot products, such as olive oil, honey, and wines. The market is open every day except Sunday and is easily accessible by public transportation or car.

Mall of Cyprus: Located in Nicosia, the Mall of Cyprus is a modern shopping center that offers a wide range of international brands, including fashion, beauty, electronics, and home goods. The mall also has a cinema, a food court, and a kids' play area.

Visitors can easily access the mall by car or public transportation.

Limassol Municipal Market: Located in the heart of Limassol, the Limassol Municipal Market is a traditional market that offers a variety of fresh produce, meats, seafood, and local products. Visitors can purchase everything from fresh fruits and vegetables to handmade ceramics and textiles. The market is open every day except Sunday and is easily accessible by public transportation or car.

Agios Athanasios Industrial Estate: Located in Limassol, the Agios Athanasios Industrial Estate is a commercial area that offers a variety of products, including furniture, electrical appliances, and building materials. Visitors can also find specialty shops that offer items such as handmade jewelry and accessories. The estate is easily accessible by car.

Chapter 5: Best Activities

Beaches and What they Offer

Cyprus is known for its stunning beaches with crystal-clear waters and golden sands. Here are some of the top beaches to visit, along with the activities you can enjoy while there:

Nissi Beach - Located in Ayia Napa, Nissi Beach is one of the most popular beaches in Cyprus. This beach offers a range of activities including water sports such as jet skiing, parasailing, and paddleboarding. Visitors can also relax on the sun loungers, take a stroll along the coast, or indulge in some delicious food and drinks at the beachfront restaurants and bars. The prices for water sports vary but usually start at around €30 per activity.

Fig Tree Bay - Situated in Protaras, Fig Tree Bay is a family-friendly beach that is known for its calm and shallow waters. Visitors can enjoy a range of water sports such as banana boat rides, pedalos, and snorkeling. There are also plenty of sun loungers and umbrellas available for hire, making it the perfect spot for a relaxing day by the sea. Prices for water sports start at around €10 per activity.

Coral Bay - Located in Paphos, Coral Bay is a Blue Flag beach that offers a range of water sports including jet skiing, parasailing, and diving. Visitors can also enjoy a leisurely swim or soak up the sun on the golden sands. There are plenty of beach bars and restaurants nearby, serving up delicious local cuisine. Prices for water sports start at around €20 per activity.

Governor's Beach - Situated between Limassol and Larnaca, Governor's Beach is a secluded spot that is perfect for those looking to escape the crowds. The beach offers a range of water sports such as kayaking and paddleboarding, as well as fishing and snorkeling.

Visitors can also explore the nearby caves and cliffs, which offer breathtaking views of the Mediterranean Sea. Prices for water sports start at around €15 per activity.

Lara Bay - Located in the Akamas Peninsula, Lara Bay is a secluded and unspoiled beach that is home to the famous Loggerhead turtles. Visitors can take a guided tour to learn more about the turtles, or simply relax on the golden sands and soak up the stunning views. There are no water sports or facilities available here, but the natural beauty of the beach makes it a must-visit spot for nature lovers.

Konnos Bay - Konnos Bay is a small and picturesque beach located in Protaras. It is surrounded by cliffs and pine trees, offering a serene and tranquil atmosphere. Visitors can enjoy a range of water sports such as jet skiing, parasailing, and windsurfing, or simply relax on the sun loungers and enjoy the scenic views. The beach also has a small restaurant that serves delicious seafood and local delicacies. Prices for water sports start at around €20 per activity.

Mackenzie Beach - Mackenzie Beach is a popular spot for locals and tourists alike, located in Larnaca. It offers a range of water sports such as kite surfing, jet skiing, and paddleboarding. Visitors can also enjoy a variety of beachfront restaurants and bars that offer local and international cuisine. The beach is also known for its vibrant nightlife scene, with several clubs and bars located nearby. Prices for water sports start at around €20 per activity.

Landa Beach - Landa Beach is located in Limassol and is known for its crystal-clear waters and soft golden sand. Visitors can enjoy a range of water sports such as jet skiing, parasailing, and paddleboarding, or simply relax on the sun loungers and soak up the sun. There are also several beachfront restaurants and bars that serve delicious food and drinks, making it the perfect spot for a day out with family and friends. Prices for water sports start at around €20 per activity.

Finikoudes Beach - Finikoudes Beach is located in the heart of Larnaca and is one of the most popular beaches on the island. It offers a range of water sports such as jet skiing, parasailing, and paddleboarding, as well as a variety of beachfront restaurants and bars that serve delicious local cuisine. Visitors can also enjoy a leisurely stroll along the promenade or take a dip in the Mediterranean Sea. Prices for water sports start at around €20 per activity.

Pissouri Beach - Pissouri Beach is located in Limassol and is known for its calm waters and stunning scenery. Visitors can enjoy a range of water sports such as kayaking, windsurfing, and paddleboarding, or simply relax on the sun loungers and soak up the sun. There are also several beachfront restaurants and bars that serve delicious food and drinks, making it the perfect spot for a day out with family and friends. Prices for water sports start at around €20 per activity.

Kapparis Beach - Kapparis Beach is located in the Famagusta area, and it's a beautiful sandy beach with crystal-clear waters. It's an ideal spot for swimming, sunbathing, and relaxing. Visitors can enjoy a range of water sports such as jet skiing, parasailing, and paddleboarding, or explore the nearby caves and cliffs. There are also several beachfront restaurants and cafes that serve delicious local cuisine. Prices for water sports start at around €20 per activity.

Alagadi Beach - Alagadi Beach is located in Kyrenia and is known for its pristine waters and stunning scenery. It's a popular spot for snorkeling and diving due to its rich marine life. Visitors can also enjoy swimming, sunbathing, and relaxing on the soft golden sand. There are no facilities available on the beach, so visitors should bring their own food and drinks. The beach is free to access, but visitors should be aware of the turtle nesting areas and avoid disturbing them.

Blue Lagoon Beach - Blue Lagoon Beach is located in the Akamas Peninsula and is known for its turquoise waters and stunning rock formations. It's an ideal spot for snorkeling and diving due to its rich marine life. Visitors can also enjoy swimming, sunbathing, and relaxing on the soft golden sand. There are no facilities available on the beach, so visitors should bring their own food and drinks. The beach is free to access, but visitors should be aware of the strong currents in the area.

Faros Beach - Faros Beach is located in Paphos and is known for its stunning views of the Mediterranean Sea. It's an ideal spot for swimming, sunbathing, and relaxing on the soft golden sand. Visitors can also enjoy a range of water sports such as jet skiing, parasailing, and paddleboarding. There are several beachfront restaurants and cafes that serve delicious local cuisine. Prices for water sports start at around €20 per activity.

Golden Beach - Golden Beach is located in the Karpas Peninsula and is known for its pristine waters and soft golden sand. It's an ideal spot for swimming, sunbathing, and relaxing in the serene atmosphere. Visitors can also enjoy a range of water sports such as jet skiing, parasailing, and paddleboarding. There are no facilities available on the beach, so visitors should bring their own food and drinks. The beach is free to access, but visitors should be aware of the turtle nesting areas and avoid disturbing them.

Historic Sites

One of the most fascinating historic sites in Cyprus is the ancient city of Kourion, located on the southwestern coast of the island. This ancient city was founded in the 13th century BC by the Mycenaean Greeks, and it played an important role in the history of Cyprus for over a thousand years.

Kourion was a thriving city during the Hellenistic, Roman, and Byzantine periods, and visitors can see a range of fascinating ruins and artifacts from each era. Among the highlights of the site are the Roman theater, which dates back to the 2nd century AD and could seat up to 3,500 spectators. Visitors can walk through the remains of the theater and imagine what it would have been like to attend a play or musical performance here. Another interesting feature of Kourion is the House of Eustolios, a well-preserved Roman villa that was built in the 4th century AD. The villa is decorated with beautiful mosaics and frescoes, and visitors can see the remains of the baths, courtyards, and other rooms that would have been used by the villa's inhabitants.

In addition to these major attractions, visitors to Kourion can explore the ruins of the city's early Christian basilica, which dates back to the 5th century AD, and the nearby stadium, which was used for athletic contests during the Roman period.

To delve deeper into the history of Kourion, visitors can also explore the on-site museum, which houses a collection of artifacts from the site and the surrounding area. These artifacts include sculptures, pottery, coins, and other items that provide insight into the daily life and culture of the people who lived in Kourion throughout its long history.

One of the most interesting things about Kourion is the way that it has been able to preserve its ancient architecture and artifacts over such a long period of time. Despite being damaged by earthquakes and other natural disasters, much of the city's original structure is still intact, giving visitors a glimpse into what life was like in Cyprus thousands of years ago.

Another fascinating aspect of Kourion is the way that it reflects the cultural influences of the many different groups of people who inhabited the city over the centuries. From the Mycenaean Greeks to the Romans and Byzantines, each era left its mark on Kourion, creating a unique blend of architectural styles and cultural traditions.

Visitors to Kourion can also take advantage of the stunning views of the Mediterranean Sea and the surrounding countryside. The city is situated on a hill overlooking the coast, providing panoramic vistas of the sea and the nearby mountains. This makes it an ideal spot for a picnic or a scenic hike, as well as a cultural excursion.

Kourion hosts a number of events throughout the year, including cultural festivals, concerts, and theatrical performances. These events provide an opportunity for visitors to experience the city's history and culture in a lively and engaging way, and to interact with locals who are passionate about preserving and sharing the city's rich heritage.

Finally, Kourion is easily accessible from the nearby city of Limassol, making it a convenient day trip for visitors to the area. Guided tours of the site are available, as well as audio guides that provide in-depth information about the various ruins and artifacts. Whether you are a history buff, a culture lover, or simply looking for a unique and unforgettable experience, a visit to Kourion is sure to be a highlight of any trip to Cyprus.

Museums and Galleries

Cyprus has a rich cultural heritage that is reflected in its museums and galleries. Visitors can explore the island's ancient past and contemporary art scene, and learn about the diverse cultural traditions that have shaped the island over the centuries. With affordable admission prices and a range of exhibitions and events, Cyprus' museums and galleries are a must-visit for anyone interested in art, history, and culture.

Museums:

Cyprus Museum: The Cyprus Museum is the oldest and largest archaeological museum in Cyprus, located in Nicosia. The museum houses a vast collection of antiquities from the Neolithic period to the Early Byzantine period, including pottery, sculpture, coins, and jewelry. Visitors can explore the galleries and learn about the island's rich history, including its ancient Greek, Roman, and Byzantine past. The museum also features a section dedicated to the island's ethnographic heritage, with exhibits on traditional costumes, tools, and everyday life. Admission to the Cyprus Museum is €4 per person.

Byzantine Museum: The Byzantine Museum is located in the Archbishop's Palace in Nicosia, and it showcases a collection of Byzantine art and artifacts from the 4th to the 19th centuries. Visitors can see exquisite mosaics, icons, frescoes, and religious objects that showcase the development of Byzantine art throughout the centuries. The museum also features a collection of medieval illuminated manuscripts, including a 10th-century gospel book that is considered one of the finest examples of Byzantine illumination.

Admission to the Byzantine Museum is €4 per person.

Leventis Municipal Museum: The Leventis Municipal Museum is located in the heart of Nicosia and is dedicated to the history and culture of the city. The museum is housed in a restored 18th-century building and features exhibits on the city's architecture, urban development, and social history. Visitors can see rare photographs, maps, and documents that chronicle the growth of Nicosia from its medieval origins to the present day. The museum also has a section dedicated to the traditional crafts and trades of Cyprus, with exhibits on weaving, pottery, and basketry. Admission to the Leventis Municipal Museum is €4 per person.

Galleries:

Gloria Gallery: The Gloria Gallery is located in the center of Nicosia and showcases contemporary art by local and international artists. The gallery hosts regular exhibitions featuring paintings, sculptures, installations, and video art. Visitors can see works by established and emerging artists, and the gallery also offers a range of educational programs and workshops. Admission to the Gloria Gallery is free.

Argo Gallery: The Argo Gallery is located in Limassol and is dedicated to promoting contemporary art from Cyprus and the wider Mediterranean region. The gallery features a range of media, including painting, sculpture, photography, and digital art. Visitors can see works by both established and emerging artists, and the gallery also hosts talks, workshops, and other events. Admission to the Argo Gallery is free.

Opus 39 Gallery: The Opus 39 Gallery is located in Larnaca and showcases contemporary art by local and international artists. The gallery features a range of media, including painting, sculpture, and photography, and hosts regular exhibitions throughout the year. Visitors can see works by established and emerging artists, and the gallery also offers a range of educational programs and workshops. Admission to the Opus 39 Gallery is free.

In addition to the museums and galleries mentioned earlier, there are many other cultural institutions in Cyprus that are worth a visit. Here are a few more:

Pierides Museum - The Pierides Museum is located in Larnaca and is housed in a restored 18th-century mansion. The museum features a collection of Cypriot art and artifacts, including pottery, sculpture, and jewelry from the Neolithic to the Roman period. Visitors can also see a collection of Byzantine icons and medieval illuminated manuscripts. Admission to the Pierides Museum is €2 per person.

Makarios Cultural Foundation - The Makarios Cultural Foundation is located in Nicosia and is dedicated to preserving the legacy of Archbishop Makarios III, the first president of Cyprus. The foundation features a museum, library, and archive, with exhibits on the life and work of

Makarios, as well as the history of Cyprus in the 20th century. Admission to the Makarios Cultural Foundation is €2 per person.

Municipal Art Gallery - The Municipal Art Gallery is located in Limassol and showcases contemporary art by local and international artists. The gallery hosts regular exhibitions featuring a range of media, including painting, sculpture, and photography. Visitors can see works by established and emerging artists, and the gallery also offers a range of educational programs and workshops. Admission to the Municipal Art Gallery is free.

Kypriaki Gonia Museum - The Kypriaki Gonia Museum is located in Larnaca and is dedicated to the traditional arts and crafts of Cyprus. The museum features exhibits on weaving, embroidery, pottery, basketry, and other traditional crafts, showcasing the skill and creativity of Cypriot artisans. Visitors can also see a collection of traditional costumes and household objects, as well as demonstrations of traditional crafts. Admission to the Kypriaki Gonia Museum is €3 per person.

St. Lazarus Ecclesiastical Museum - The St. Lazarus Ecclesiastical Museum is located in Larnaca and is housed in a

9th-century Byzantine church. The museum features a collection of religious artifacts, including icons, vestments, and liturgical objects, as well as exhibits on the history and architecture of the church. Visitors can also explore the church itself, with its beautiful frescoes and ornate decorations. Admission to the St. Lazarus Ecclesiastical Museum is €2 per person.

Paphos Archaeological Park - The Paphos Archaeological Park is located in Paphos and features a collection of ancient ruins dating back to the Roman period. Visitors can explore the remains of a Roman villa, including its beautiful mosaics, as well as the ancient theater and the Tombs of the Kings. The park also features a museum with exhibits on the history of Paphos and its ancient past. Admission to the Paphos Archaeological Park is €4.50 per person.

Museum of Kyrenia - The Museum of Kyrenia is located in the town of Kyrenia and is housed in a 16th-century castle. The museum features exhibits on the history of Kyrenia and the wider region, including ancient artifacts, medieval weapons, and Ottoman-era ceramics. Visitors can also explore the castle itself, with its stunning views of the harbor and the Mediterranean Sea.

Admission to the Museum of Kyrenia is €4 per person.

Outdoor Activities

Cyprus is a fantastic destination for outdoor enthusiasts of all ages, interests, and fitness levels. From hiking and cycling to water sports and adventure activities, there's something for everyone. Here are some ideas for outdoor activities that cater to singles, couples, and families:

For Singles:

Hiking: Cyprus has several well-marked trails that offer stunning views of the coastline, mountains, and forests. Some popular hiking routes include the Aphrodite Trail, Akamas Peninsula, and Troodos Mountains.

Cycling: With a network of cycle paths and quiet roads, Cyprus is an excellent destination for cycling. You can rent a bike from a local shop or join a guided cycling tour that explores the countryside or coastal areas.

Water sports: Whether it's windsurfing, kiteboarding, paddleboarding, or jet skiing, there are plenty of water sports to try in Cyprus. You can book a lesson or rent equipment from a local water sports center.

For Couples:

Wine tasting: Cyprus has a long history of wine production, and there are many wineries and vineyards to visit. You can take a guided tour that includes tastings and food pairings.

Scuba diving: With crystal-clear waters and abundant marine life, Cyprus is a top destination for scuba diving. You can take a beginner course or join a guided dive to explore the wrecks, reefs, and caves.

Sunset cruise: Enjoy a romantic evening on a sunset cruise that takes you along the coast or to a secluded bay. You can choose from a private or group tour that includes drinks and snacks.

For Families:

Beach activities: With miles of sandy beaches and calm waters, Cyprus is ideal for families with young children.

You can swim, sunbathe, build sandcastles, and play beach games.

Nature walks: Cyprus has several nature reserves and parks that offer easy walking trails suitable for families. You can spot local flora and fauna, enjoy a picnic, or visit a wildlife sanctuary.

Adventure parks: Cyprus has several adventure parks that offer a range of activities such as zip-lining, rope courses, and climbing walls. You can join a guided tour or purchase a day pass that includes all activities.

Organizing Outdoor Activities: Many outdoor activities in Cyprus are organized by local tour operators or activity centers. Visitors can book these activities online, at the activity center, or through their hotel concierge. Depending on the activity, visitors may need to bring their equipment, such as hiking boots or swimwear, or rent equipment from the activity center. Visitors should also check the weather forecast and dress appropriately for the activity.

Participating in Outdoor Activities: Visitors should follow the safety instructions and guidelines provided by the activity center or tour operator. They should also inform the center of any medical conditions or allergies that may affect their participation. Visitors should arrive on time, with any necessary documents or waivers signed. Finally, visitors should respect the environment and local customs and avoid any behavior that may harm the surroundings or offend the locals.

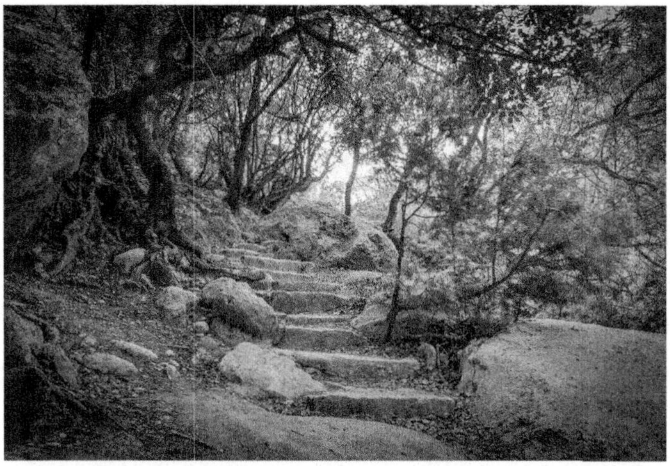

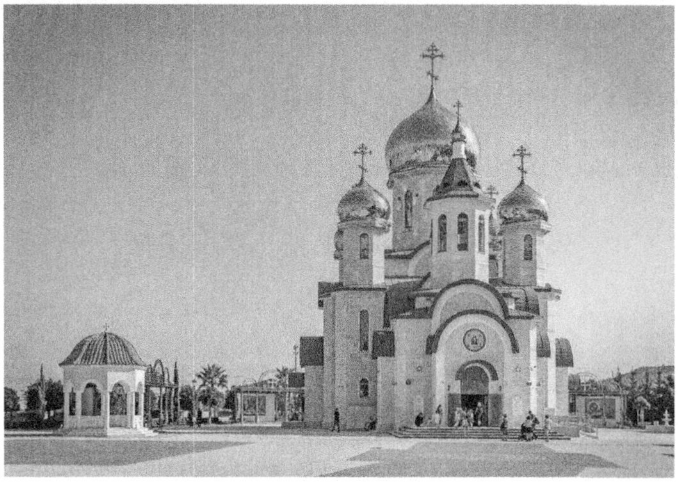

Chapter 6: Food and Drink

Cypriot Cuisine

Cypriot cuisine is a combination of traditional Mediterranean and Middle Eastern flavors. Cyprus, being an island country, has a unique cuisine that is influenced by its location and history. The island has a rich agricultural tradition, and its cuisine features fresh ingredients such as vegetables, fruits, herbs, and seafood.

One of the most popular dishes in Cypriot cuisine is "meze," which is a selection of small dishes served together, similar to Spanish tapas.

Meze typically includes dishes like hummus, tzatziki, olives, grilled halloumi cheese, keftedes (meatballs), and souvlaki (grilled meat skewers). Another popular dish is kleftiko, which is slow-cooked lamb or goat meat that is marinated with herbs and spices, then wrapped in parchment paper and baked in a clay oven.

Fish is also a common ingredient in Cypriot cuisine, with popular dishes like grilled octopus, squid stew, and fried calamari. The island's coastline is rich in seafood, and it is typically prepared with herbs, lemon, and olive oil. Vegetables like tomatoes, eggplants, and peppers are also widely used in Cypriot dishes. One example is gemista, which is stuffed peppers or tomatoes with rice, vegetables, and herbs.

Nutritionally, Cypriot cuisine is generally considered to be healthy due to its emphasis on fresh ingredients and simple preparation methods. Olive oil is a staple in the cuisine, and it is a good source of healthy monounsaturated fats. Many dishes also include legumes like chickpeas and lentils, which are high in protein and fiber. Fish dishes are a good source of omega-3 fatty acids, which are important for heart health.

Overall, Cypriot cuisine is a delicious and healthy combination of Mediterranean and Middle Eastern flavors. Its emphasis on fresh ingredients and simple preparation methods make it a great choice for those looking for a healthy and flavorful cuisine.

Popular Dishes and Drinks

Popular Cypriot Dishes:

Souvlaki: Souvlaki is a popular Cypriot dish made with marinated meat (usually pork, chicken, or lamb) that is grilled on skewers. The meat is usually served with pita bread, chopped onions, tomatoes, and a yogurt sauce called tzatziki. Souvlaki is a great source of protein and can be a healthy meal if prepared with lean meat and served with plenty of vegetables.

Moussaka: Moussaka is a dish made with layers of sliced potatoes, eggplant, and ground meat (usually beef or lamb) that are baked in a tomato sauce and topped with a creamy bechamel sauce. Moussaka is a rich and hearty dish that is high in calories and fat, but it also provides a good source of protein and carbohydrates.

Halloumi: Halloumi is a semi-hard cheese that is made from a mixture of goat's and sheep's milk. It has a salty and slightly tangy flavor, and it is often served grilled or fried. Halloumi is a good source of calcium and protein, but it is also high in fat and sodium.

Stifado: Stifado is a stew made with beef or rabbit meat that is slow-cooked with onions, tomatoes, and a variety of spices (such as cinnamon, cloves, and bay leaves). Stifado is a flavorful and filling dish that is high in protein and nutrients.

Cypriot Drinks:

Zivania: Zivania is a traditional Cypriot spirit made from distilled grape pomace. It has a strong flavor and a high alcohol content (usually around 45-50%). Zivania is often served as a digestif after a meal, and it is also used in cooking.

Commandaria: Commandaria is a sweet dessert wine that is made from sun-dried grapes. It has a rich, fruity flavor and a high sugar content. Commandaria is often served with desserts or cheese.

Frappe: Frappe is a popular Cypriot coffee drink that is made by mixing instant coffee, sugar, and water with a hand-held mixer. The mixture is then poured over ice and topped with milk. Frappe is a refreshing and energizing drink that is popular throughout Cyprus, especially during the hot summer months.

Lemonade: Lemonade is a refreshing drink that is made with freshly squeezed lemons, water, and sugar. It is a popular drink in Cyprus, especially during the summer months when temperatures can reach 40°C. Lemonade is a great source of vitamin C and antioxidants, and it can also help to hydrate the body.

Keo Beer: Keo Beer is a popular beer in Cyprus that is brewed locally. It is a light, refreshing beer that is perfect for hot summer days. Keo Beer is often served with meze, a selection of small dishes that are typically served as appetizers.

Cypriot Coffee: Cypriot coffee is a strong and flavorful coffee that is brewed using finely ground coffee beans and a traditional briki (a small copper or brass pot). The coffee is brewed with water and sugar, and it is served unfiltered. Cypriot coffee is often enjoyed with a small glass of water and a piece of lokum (Turkish delight).

Commandaria liqueur: Commandaria liqueur is a sweet and syrupy liqueur that is made from the same sun-dried grapes used to make Commandaria wine. It has a rich, fruity flavor and is often served as a digestif after a meal.

Anari: Anari is a traditional Cypriot cheese made from the whey left over from making halloumi. It has a mild, creamy flavor and a crumbly texture. Anari is often served as a dessert cheese, either on its own or with honey and nuts.

Restaurants and Cafes

There are plenty of great restaurants and cafes in Cyprus to choose from, whether you're in the mood for traditional Cypriot cuisine or a healthy snack.

Here are some Cypriot restaurants and cafes worth checking out:

Zanettos - Located in Nicosia, Zanettos is a traditional Cypriot tavern that serves authentic local cuisine. Their menu includes dishes like grilled halloumi, souvlaki, and moussaka. The restaurant has a cozy atmosphere with indoor and outdoor seating options. Prices are reasonable, with dishes ranging from €8-€15.

To Katoi - To Katoi is a family-run restaurant in Limassol that specializes in meze, a selection of small dishes that are shared among diners. The menu includes a variety of meat, seafood, and vegetarian options. The restaurant has a rustic, traditional feel, with both indoor and outdoor seating. Prices for meze start at €20 per person.

Militzis - Militzis is another popular meze restaurant in Limassol. They offer a wide selection of traditional Cypriot dishes, including grilled meat, fish, and vegetarian options. The restaurant has a spacious outdoor terrace with views of the sea. Prices for meze start at €19 per person.

As for cafes:

Piatsa Gourounaki - Piatsa Gourounaki is a popular cafe chain in Cyprus with locations in Nicosia, Limassol, and Larnaca. They specialize in traditional Greek and Cypriot coffee, as well as pastries and light snacks. Prices are affordable, with coffee starting at €2 and pastries starting at €1.

Croissanterie - Croissanterie is a European-style cafe with locations in

Limassol and Nicosia. They offer a variety of breakfast items, sandwiches, salads, and pastries. The cafe has a cozy atmosphere with indoor and outdoor seating options. Prices are reasonable, with items starting at €3.

Caffe Nero - Caffe Nero is a chain coffee shop with locations throughout Cyprus. They offer a variety of coffee drinks, teas, and pastries. The cafe has a modern, upscale feel with indoor and outdoor seating options. Prices are similar to other coffee shop chains, with coffee starting at €2.5 and pastries starting at €1.5.

Kafenio - Kafenio is a traditional Cypriot cafe located in Larnaca. They serve authentic coffee and a variety of local pastries, such as loukoumades and bourekia. The cafe has a cozy, old-fashioned feel with indoor and outdoor seating options. Prices are affordable, with coffee starting at €2 and pastries starting at €1.

Salad Box - Salad Box is a healthy eating cafe chain with locations in Limassol, Nicosia, and Larnaca. They offer a variety of salads, wraps, and smoothies made with fresh, locally sourced ingredients. The cafe has a modern, bright feel with indoor and outdoor seating options. Prices are reasonable, with salads starting at €6 and smoothies starting at €3.

Mokka Specialty Coffee - Mokka Specialty Coffee is a specialty coffee shop located in Nicosia. They offer a variety of coffee drinks, including espresso-based drinks and pour-overs, as well as a selection of pastries and light bites. The cafe has a stylish, minimalist feel with indoor and outdoor seating options. Prices are on the higher end, with coffee starting at €3.5 and pastries starting at €2.

Chapter 7: Practical Information

Health and Safety

When visiting Cyprus, it's essential to be aware of the health and safety measures in place to ensure a safe and enjoyable stay.

Firstly, it's important to note that Cyprus has a good standard of healthcare facilities. Public hospitals and clinics are available throughout the island, while private healthcare options are also available. However, visitors are advised to have comprehensive travel insurance that covers medical expenses in case of emergencies.

In terms of safety, Cyprus is considered a relatively safe destination. However, visitors should take standard precautions such as avoiding walking alone at night in unfamiliar areas, keeping an eye on personal belongings, and taking care when driving on the island's roads.

In case of emergency, visitors can dial 112, the European emergency number, to reach the police, ambulance, or fire services. The Cyprus Civil Defence department is responsible for dealing with emergencies and natural disasters such as earthquakes, floods, and forest fires. They can be contacted on 112 or 199.

If you need medical assistance, the following emergency response units are available:

Ambulance services - dial 112 or 199
General emergency services - dial 112 or 199

Cyprus Red Cross - provides first aid training, ambulance services, blood donation, and other emergency services. Contact number: +357 22 818 181

Poison Control Center - dial 1401

Here are some hospitals in Cyprus and their locations:

Nicosia General Hospital - Located in the capital city of Nicosia, it is the largest hospital in Cyprus and provides general medical services, emergency services, and specialist services. Visitors can access it by car or public transportation.

Limassol General Hospital - Located in the city of Limassol, it provides general medical services, emergency services, and specialist services. Visitors can access it by car or public transportation.

Larnaca General Hospital - Located in the city of Larnaca, it provides general medical services, emergency services, and specialist services. Visitors can access it by car or public transportation.

Paphos General Hospital - Located in the city of Paphos, it provides general medical services, emergency services, and specialist services. Visitors can access it by car or public transportation.

Famagusta General Hospital - Located in the city of Famagusta, it provides general medical services, emergency services, and specialist services. Visitors can access it by car or public transportation.

Makarios Hospital - Located in the capital city of Nicosia, it is a children's hospital that provides pediatric medical services, including emergency services and specialist services. Visitors can access it by car or public transportation.

American Medical Center - Located in Nicosia, it is a private hospital that provides medical services for both locals and foreigners. Visitors can access it by car or public transportation.

Mediterranean Hospital of Cyprus - Located in Limassol, it is a private hospital that provides medical services for both locals and foreigners. Visitors can access it by car or public transportation.

Visitors should research the hospitals in their vicinity before traveling to Cyprus to ensure they know where to go in case of a medical emergency. It's also recommended to keep a list of emergency contact numbers, including the embassy of your home country, in case of any unforeseen situations.

Communication and Internet

Communication and Internet services in Cyprus are well-developed, making it easy for visitors to stay connected during their trip. Here are some of the services available for visitors:

Mobile Networks: There are three main mobile network providers in Cyprus, namely MTN, CYTA, and Primetel. Visitors can purchase prepaid SIM cards from any of these providers at reasonable rates. The cost of a SIM card ranges from €5-€10, and you'll need to provide your passport or ID to activate it.

Wi-Fi Hotspots: Wi-Fi hotspots are available in most hotels, cafes, and public places in Cyprus. Many restaurants and cafes offer free Wi-Fi to customers, and there are also several public Wi-Fi hotspots in cities like Nicosia, Limassol, and Larnaca.

Internet Cafes: Internet cafes are also available in Cyprus, where visitors can use the internet for a fee. The rates vary depending on the location and the amount of time you use the internet.

Roaming: Visitors can also use their mobile phone plan's roaming feature to stay connected while in Cyprus. However, roaming charges can be expensive, so it's best to check with your mobile network provider to see if they offer any roaming packages.

Free Wi-Fi Hotspots: There are several locations in Cyprus where visitors can access free Wi-Fi hotspots. For example, the public libraries in Nicosia and Limassol offer free Wi-Fi to visitors, as do many public parks and squares.

Paid Wi-Fi Hotspots: There are also paid Wi-Fi hotspots available in some areas of Cyprus. These can be found in shopping malls, airports, and other public places. The cost varies depending on the location and the amount of time you use the internet.

It's worth noting that while Cyprus has excellent communication and internet services, there may be some areas of the country where internet connectivity is slower or less reliable. This is especially true in more rural areas or on smaller islands, where infrastructure may be less developed. However, in general, most visitors should have no trouble staying connected.

If you're planning to rely on your mobile phone while in Cyprus, it's a good idea to check with your mobile network provider to ensure that your phone is compatible with the local networks. You may need to unlock your phone before you can use a local SIM card.

Another important thing to keep in mind is that Cyprus is in the Eastern European Time Zone (EET), which is two hours ahead of Coordinated Universal Time (UTC+2). This means that if you're calling or texting people in another time zone, you'll need to be mindful of the time difference

Conclusion

Final Thoughts

Cyprus is a stunning destination that offers a blend of ancient history, picturesque landscapes, and a Mediterranean lifestyle. With its beautiful beaches, charming villages, and delicious cuisine, Cyprus has something to offer every type of traveler. From exploring the historic landmarks to enjoying the warm sunshine on the sandy shores, visitors to Cyprus will not be disappointed. It's definitely worth considering for your next holiday destination.

If you're interested in outdoor activities like hiking and diving or prefer to relax and soak up the culture, Cyprus has a lot to offer. The island's rich history is visible everywhere, from the ancient ruins to the traditional villages, and the local cuisine is a delicious fusion of Greek, Turkish, and Middle Eastern flavors. The Cypriot people are friendly and welcoming, making visitors feel right at home.

When planning a trip to Cyprus, be sure to explore both the northern and southern parts of the island. The south is known for its bustling cities, stunning beaches, and historical sites, while the north is more laid-back with a quieter atmosphere and a unique mix of Greek and Turkish cultures. It's important to note that there is a political divide between the two sides of the island, and visitors should be respectful of local customs and sensitivities.

In terms of the best time to visit, Cyprus is a year-round destination. The peak tourist season is during the summer months (June to August), when the weather is hot and sunny, and the beaches are in full swing. However, if you prefer a quieter vacation, consider visiting in the shoulder seasons of spring (March to May) and autumn (September to November), when the temperatures are milder and the crowds are fewer.

When it comes to getting around Cyprus, renting a car is the most convenient option, as public transportation can be limited outside of the main cities. The roads are generally well-maintained, and driving is on the left-hand side, as in the UK.

In terms of accommodation, Cyprus offers a wide range of options to suit every budget and preference, from luxury hotels and resorts to traditional guesthouses and self-catering apartments.

Useful Resources to plan your trip to Cyprus

Visit Cyprus - Official tourism website of Cyprus provides comprehensive information on attractions, accommodation, events, and activities.

Cyprus Tourism Organisation - The national tourism organization of Cyprus, providing information on places to visit, activities, and events.

Cyprus Maps - A collection of maps of Cyprus that you can use to plan your travel routes and activities.

Cyprus Airports - Information on the two main airports in Cyprus, Larnaca and Paphos, including flight schedules and transportation options.

Cyprus Car Rental - Renting a car is the best way to explore Cyprus. This website provides information on car rental companies, prices, and booking.

Cyprus Public Transport - Information on public transportation in Cyprus, including bus schedules, routes, and fares.

Cyprus Weather - A detailed weather forecast for Cyprus, including temperature, precipitation, and wind conditions.

Cyprus Currency - Information on the currency used in Cyprus and exchange rates.

Cyprus Embassy - Contact information for the Cyprus embassy in your country if you need assistance with visas or other travel-related issues.

Cyprus Travel Forum - A community of travelers discussing their experiences, tips, and advice for traveling in Cyprus.

Cyprus Food and Drink - A guide to the best food and drink in Cyprus, including traditional Cypriot dishes and where to find them.

Cyprus Beaches - Information on the best beaches in Cyprus, including their features, activities, and amenities.

Cyprus Archaeological Sites - A guide to the archaeological sites in Cyprus, including their history and significance.

Cyprus Wine Routes - Information on the wine routes in Cyprus, including the vineyards, wineries, and wine tasting experiences.

Cyprus Festivals and Events - A calendar of festivals and events in Cyprus throughout the year, including cultural, religious, and sporting events.

Cyprus National Parks - Information on the national parks in Cyprus, including hiking trails, picnic areas, and wildlife.

Cyprus Travel Insurance - Information on travel insurance options for your trip to Cyprus.

Cyprus Emergency Services - Contact information for emergency services in Cyprus, including police, ambulance, and fire department.

Cyprus Language and Culture - A guide to the language and culture of Cyprus, including common phrases, customs, and traditions.

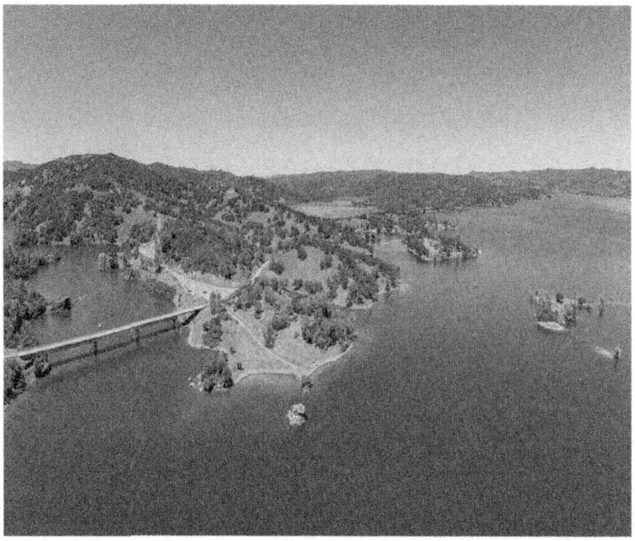

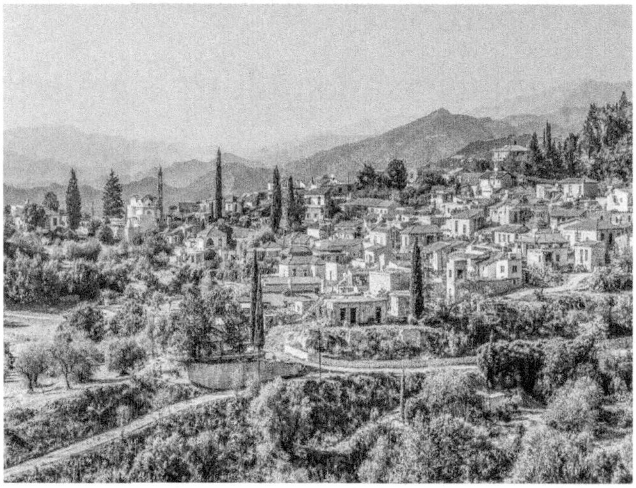